Flying with
Flight Simulator

Be an expert!

The **Be an expert!** series consists of books which enable you to teach yourself in an easy and straightforward way how to work with a computer program.

You simply follow the theory and the practical exercises and ... No trouble! It works! This series aims at being both pleasant and educational.

Also published in this series:

Theo van Keulen

Flying with
Flight Simulator
Be an expert!

Prisma *Be an expert!* first published in Great Britain by

Het Spectrum
P.O. Box 2996
London N5 2TA London

Translation: George Hall
Production: LINE UP text productions

For the English translation
© 1995 Uitgeverij Het Spectrum B.V., Utrecht

ISBN 1 85365 312 8

British Library Cataloguing-in-Publication Data.
A catalogue record for this book is available from the British Library.

Contents

Introduction

Throughout history, people have dreamt of being able to fly like birds. It remained a dream for thousands of years (unless you believe that people are descended from spacemen as some scientists claim). But at the beginning of this century, in 1909 on the beach at Kitty Hawk in North Carolina in the USA, a small flying machine rose into the air. This machine was built by the Wright brothers, and the dream had become reality!

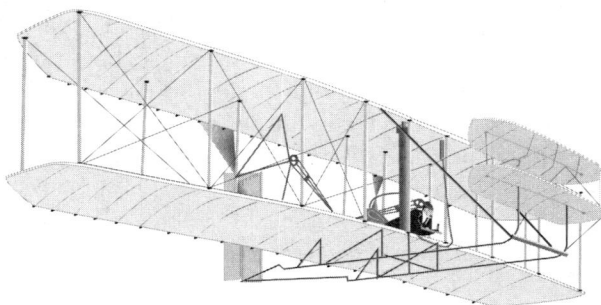

A lot has happened since this first motorised flight. The Wright brothers had to learn how to steer the flying machine by trial and error. If the machine was damaged due to a mistake while landing, they were sometimes busy for weeks on end trying to repair the damage. That was, of course, an expensive business.

Why use flight simulators?

Modern aeroplanes are a good deal more complex than the first models. For this reason, pilots are given training which makes use of **flight simulators**. These devices are very similar to the inside of the cockpit. Some simulators represent the real situation to such an extent that you forget that you are not actually in an aeroplane. In fact, that is the whole intention.

This kind of simulator is an excellent aid to pilots for the simple reason that you can practise actions which are difficult to carry out in a real plane. For instance, an engine failure can be simulated in a real plane by closing the fuel supply, but a short circuit or even fire in the engines cannot be carried out in real life. It's much too dangerous and also ruins the planes.

Another advantage of the simulator is that you can stop it for a while and explain exactly what is happening to the trainees. Of course, you cannot do this in a real plane. Gravity has been invented.

The simulator we shall deal with in this book is the Microsoft **Flight Simulator version 5.0**. It is not as complicated as the simulator used to train pilots who operate large line flights, but it does give a good idea of how to fly a small single-engine aeroplane. You can even select one of a number of planes.

The scope of this book

As mentioned, this book deals with the Microsoft Flight Simulator version 5.0. We presume that the program has been installed on your computer. If that is not the case, consult the manual or ask some-one else who knows a bit more about computers to help you.

MS-DOS

We also presume that you know how to switch the computer on and off and how to work with MS-DOS to a certain extent.

The screen images in this book

The screen images in this book have been made using a computer with a so-called **SVGA** graphic card (Super VGA). If you have a different graphic card in your computer, such as **VGA** or **EGA** for example, the images on your screen will look a little different. In practice, this should cause no problems. If there are any large differences between the imag-es produced by these various graphic cards, we shall say so.

Joystick, keyboard or mouse?

There are three ways to operate the Flight Simulator: by means of the joystick(s), by means of the keyboard, or using the mouse. In this book, we

shall use the **keyboard** in principle, because this
provides the best method of explaining all the functions. Moreover, not everybody has a joystick. In
general, the mouse is not very convenient for operating the Flight Simulator, although it is very suitable
for selecting menus and menu options. Throughout
this book, we shall frequently indicate the various
methods which can be applied.

When talking about key combinations, we mean
the following. If you see for example: 'Press **Alt-E**',
this means that you should press and hold down the
Alt key and then press the **E** key; then release both
keys.

By pressing the **right** mouse button, you can switch
back and forth between operating the menus and
operating the Flight Simulator. If the mouse pointer
(the slanting arrow on the screen) is displayed, you
can operate the menus. When you press the **right**
mouse button, the mouse pointer disappears and
you can operate the Flight Simulator. We shall
return to this topic in chapter 2.

1   A little theory

Before taking off, it might be handy to know something about the principles of flying. This might help you understand why the aeroplane reacts in a particular way when actually 'in the air'. Many people think that an aeroplane can fly because of the **engine**. This is not true of course. A glider or a paper aeroplane can also fly and remain in the air for a lengthy period of time.

How does a plane fly?

The wings

The wings of a plane are not just flat planks. They have a special shape. This special shape is responsible for the fact that, as the aeroplane moves forwards, underpressure is created **above** the wing and overpressure is created **under** the wing. This means that the air pressure pushes the wing upwards. This is referred to as **lift**. If there is sufficient speed, the lift becomes large enough to carry the whole weight of the aeroplane. And how do we attain this speed? Exactly, by running the engines. The engines make the speed, the wings make the lift.

The lift

If you look at the figure overleaf, you can get an idea of how the lift is created. The figure shows a cross-section of the wing. The air, as it approaches the front of the wing, is split into two main streams. One stream goes over the wing, the other goes under. If you have a good look, you will see that the air which goes over the top of the wing has to travel further than the air which goes under. This is because the top of the wing is rounded. The streams have to join together again at the back of the wing (Nature abhors a vacuum) which means that the air above the wing becomes more 'stretched out'; it has to travel faster. Because of this, it is thinner as it were. It has **less pressure**.

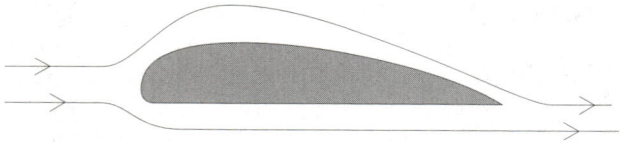

The airstreams round the wing profile

This underpressure is not solely responsible for the lift. The wing itself meets the oncoming air at a certain angle. This also produces **higher pressure** on the underside of the wing, producing upwards force. These two combined forces, the higher pressure on the underside and the underpressure above the wing produce the upwards lift. Roughly two thirds of the lift is caused by the underpressure above the wing and the remaining third is caused by the higher pressure resulting from the angle of the wing.

The propeller

The propeller blades of a plane have roughly the same shape (in cross-section) as the wings. You can regard them as two revolving wings which also produce lift. This lift is not in an upwards direction; it is in a **forwards direction**. The propeller 'pulls' the aeroplane forwards.

The parts of the aeroplane

The following figure shows the parts of the aeroplane. We have already discussed the wings and the propeller.

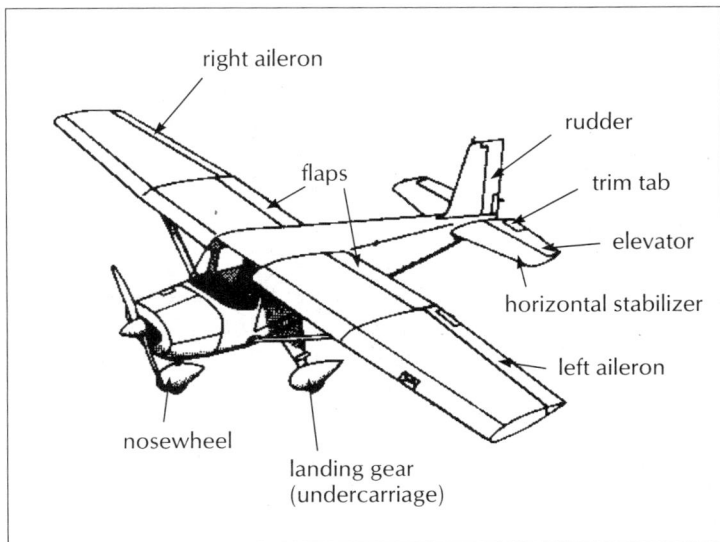

right aileron

rudder

flaps

trim tab

elevator

horizontal stabilizer

left aileron

nosewheel

landing gear
(undercarriage)

The parts of the aeroplane

Guiding the plane

The **elevator** is linked to the steering wheel in the plane. This steering wheel is referred to as the **control yoke**. If you push the control yoke forwards, the elevator is moved downwards. This results in the tail of the aeroplane rising which, in turn, means that the nose of the plane points downwards. If you pull the control yoke backwards, the elevator rises. The plane then begins to 'climb'.

You operate the **ailerons** by turning the control yoke. If you turn it to the left, the left aileron rises and the right aileron moves downwards. This results in the plane banking over to the left; thus, you in fact turn left. By turning the control yoke to the right, the reverse process occurs.

There is also the **rudder**. We shall deal with this below.

The pedals

There are two pedals in the plane and these have varying functions. Among other things, they are linked to the **rudder**. By pressing the left or the right pedal, the rudder is moved to the left or the right. If you do this along with turning the control yoke to move the ailerons, the plane will then make a turn in an evenly balanced way. This may seem to be a bit complicated, but the ailerons and the rudder are linked in the simulator so that you can always make an even, co-ordinated turn.

The same two pedals are also linked to the **nose-wheel** so that you can make a turn when on the ground. If you press the left pedal, the nosewheel turns to the left, which also turns the entire plane to the left. Turning the nosewheel to the right will turn the plane to the right.

The third pedal function is **braking**. When on the ground, press the top part of the pedals to activate the brakes. The brakes are on the two landing gear wheels; there is no brake on the nose wheel. Of course, the brakes only work when you are on the ground.

The flaps

The **flaps** are situated at the back of the wings, next to the body (fuselage) of the aircraft. Normally, these flaps are up, which means they conform to the shape of the wing. When you come to land, you use the flaps to be able to fly more slowly. In that case, the flaps are turned downwards and are also moved backwards - they extend out of the wing. Because they stick out, the **surface area** of the wings is **increased**: the wings become larger. This produces more lift. And because the flaps **turn downwards**, the **rounding** of the wings is **increased**. This produces not only more lift but also more air resistance. All in all, the plane flies more slowly which is just what's needed when you are going to land.

You can also use the flaps when taking off the aircraft, although you must not turn them downwards by more than 10 degrees. This produces more lift at a slower speed so that a shorter runway is required.

In the cockpit

Before taking off, we shall examine the most important flying instruments. If you look straight ahead at the instrument panel, you will see six instruments:

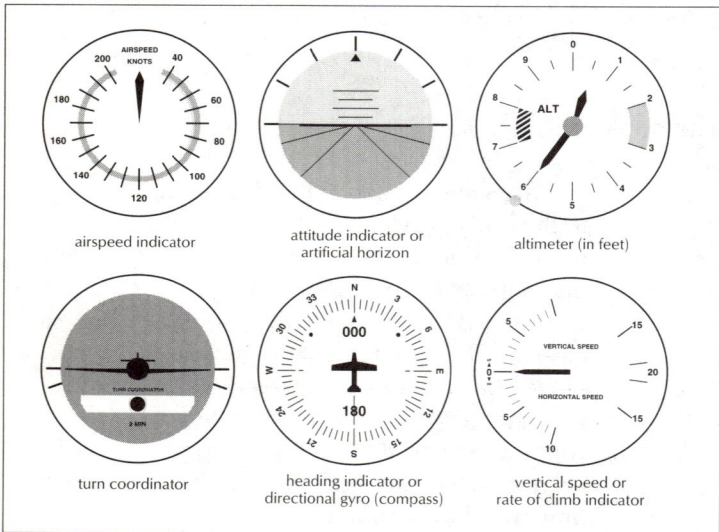

airspeed indicator	attitude indicator or artificial horizon	altimeter (in feet)
turn coordinator	heading indicator or directional gyro (compass)	vertical speed or rate of climb indicator

The six most important instruments

The airspeed indicator

The airspeed indicator is shown in the upper left-hand corner. In aviation, speed is generally measured in **knots**. The smallest number shown on the airspeed indicator of the Cessna - the plane in which we shall fly - is 40 knots. A knot is a little more than one mile per hour. The highest number displayed is 200 knots, but the maximum speed permitted is just under 180 knots. A red line on the airspeed indicator indicates this.

The artificial horizon

The meter next to the airspeed indicator is the **artificial horizon**, also known as the attitude indicator. This instrument shows the position of the aircraft in relation to the horizon. Normally, you will be able to see the horizon by simply looking through the window. But if you fly through clouds or in the dark, you will need to use the artificial horizon along with other instruments to determine the position of the plane. The white line, roughly in the middle of the dial, represents the wings. The upper blue section represents the air and the lower part, in brown, represents the ground. A white triangle is shown at the top of the dial. This indicates the number of degrees of inclination or 'bank' at which the aircraft is currently flying. If the triangle is at the central white point, the wings are completely horizontal. The next dot indicates an inclination of 10 degrees, the others indicate 20, 30, 60 and 90 degrees.

The altimeter

The next meter which we shall deal with is the **altimeter**. This instrument is to the right of the artificial horizon. Altitude is normally measured in feet in aviation. If you examine the altimeter, you will see that it has two hands just like a clock. The large hand represents the **hundreds** and the small hand represents the **thousands**. Thus, the first altimeter shown below indicates a height of 3000 feet. See if you can read the second altimeter.

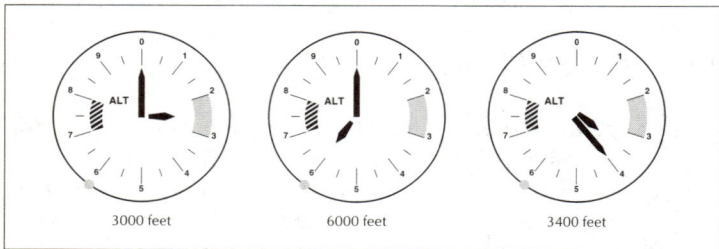

Three values on the altimeter

Exactly, the second altimeter indicates that you are flying at a height of 6000 feet. And the third one? It indicates that you are flying at a height of 3400 feet. In fact, the altimeter is a special kind of **barometer**. It measures air pressure. The higher up you are, the smaller the air pressure. In this way, you can find out how high you are. The altimeter reads the air pressure and converts the result to feet.

Using the altimeter does bring one small problem. Due to the fact that the air pressure on the ground is not always the same (it depends on the weather), you have to adjust the altimeter a little. The button

to the immediate left of the altimeter enables you to
do this. The air traffic control informs you of the
altimeter setting and you can adjust the meter
yourself. If there is no air traffic control or weather
station, specify the height of the airfield yourself.
The height of the airfield (above sea level) is shown
on the map you have with you in the cockpit.

The turn coordinator

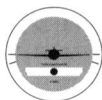

If we now look at the lower left-hand corner of the
instrument panel, we see the **turn coordinator**.
The shape of an aeroplane is shown with a diagonal
stripe under each wing. The letters L and R (for left
and right) are also shown. If you turn leftwards and
the wing of the plane forms one line with the stripe
above the L, it will take two minutes to make a turn
of 360 degrees, a complete circle. This is referred to
as a **standard rate turn**.

The same instrument also displays a black ball. If
you make sure that this ball stays in the middle of
the dial between the two thin stripes, the turn will
be well **coordinated**. This means you will make a
perfect turn and will not slip or skid, in other words
you will keep to the planned course of the turn.

The heading indicator or directional gyro

The instrument under the artificial horizon is the
heading indicator or **directional gyro**. This indicates the direction in which you are flying. The dial
is divided into 360 degrees. If you fly a heading of

360 degrees (in other words, 000 degrees), you fly towards the north. If you fly in the opposite direction, your course is 180 degrees. The east is 90 degrees and the west is 270 degrees.

The vertical speed or rate of climb indicator

The instrument to the right of the heading indicator is the **vertical speed indicator (VSI) or rate of climb indicator**. This instrument indeed shows the rate of vertical change per minute in feet. If the needle is on the upper number 5, you are climbing at a rate of 500 feet per minute. If it is on the lower number 10, you are descending at 1000 feet per minute.

The control position indicators

Between the artificial horizon and the altimeter, there are three 'rulers': two horizontal and one vertical. The top horizontal ruler, the **aileron position indicator** shows the current position of the ailerons. The bottom horizontal ruler, the **rudder position indicator** shows the current rudder position. In the Flight Simulator, they are linked so that they will normally move simultaneously. The vertical ruler, the **elevator position indicator** shows the current elevator position. This indicator is not present in a normal aeroplane because you can always feel the amount of force you exert on the elevator. But on the computer, you cannot feel this, so it is necessary to have an instrument to indicate it. Accordingly, you can get a good idea of the position of the air-craft guiding components.

These are the most important instruments. The instrument panel displays much more information but that will be discussed further on in the book.

2   Our first flight

After all this theory, you will want to take off. OK, let's go!

Starting up the Flight Simulator

When you first switch on the computer, you will see this on your screen:

```
C:\>_
```

That is the 'DOS-prompt', as you will probably know.

Now type: **cd fltsim5** and press the **Enter** key. This command switches you to the directory in which the Flight Simulator is situated.

Then type: **fs5** and press the **Enter** key again. This command starts up the Flight Simulator.

A plane, a Learjet, is shown above a city. Then the
Flight Simulator screen appears:

The runway at Meigs Field airport, Chicago

The simulator screen

You are now in the cockpit of your aeroplane on
the runway at Meigs Field airport, Chicago, USA.
The upper section of the screen is the window
through which you see the surroundings, the lower
section is the instrument panel display.

The instruments

See if you recognise the instruments we dealt with
in the previous chapter. You will see that the airspeed indicator shows zero at the moment. We are
still on the ground. The altimeter indicates a height
of a little less than 600 feet. This is due to the fact
that Meigs Field lies at a height of 593 feet above
sea level. The directional indicator shows 000
degrees. This means that the aircraft is pointing
exactly northwards at this moment.

The menus

The bar along the top of the screen is the **menu bar**.
Menus are available here although they are currently concealed. You can open them in two ways:

1. Using the **mouse**. If the mouse pointer is visible
    (if not press the **right** mouse button), move it to
    a word on the menu bar and click on it by press-
    ing the left mouse button.
2. Using the **Alt** key. Press the **Alt** key to activate
    the menu bar and then press the underlined let-
    ter of one of the menus shown on the menu bar.

When a menu has been opened, you can select
one of the options by clicking on it using the
mouse. You can also use the ↓ or ↑ cursor keys to
move to it and then press **Enter**. You can also press
the underlined letter of the required option.

Press the **Alt** key and then the **O**. The **Options** menu appears:

```
Options
✓Normal Flight
 Entertainment...

 Quick Practice...
 Flight Instruction...
 Land Me              X

 Instant Replay...
 Video Recorder...
 Flight Analysis...
 Logbook...

 Situations...
 Save Situation...    ;
 Reset Situation      Ctrl PrtSc

 Aircraft...

 Simulator Info...
 Preferences...

 Exit...              Ctrl Break
```

The Options menu

To close the menu, press the **Esc** key.

If you find the menu bar a bit of a nuisance when flying, you can press the **Esc** key to remove it from the screen. If you want to recall it, press the Esc key once again.

A good demonstration first

Before taking off ourselves, we shall view a demonstration flight first.

Open the **Options** menu by means of the mouse or by pressing **Alt-O**. The word **Preferences** is shown on the second last line.

Select **Preferences**. A submenu appears.

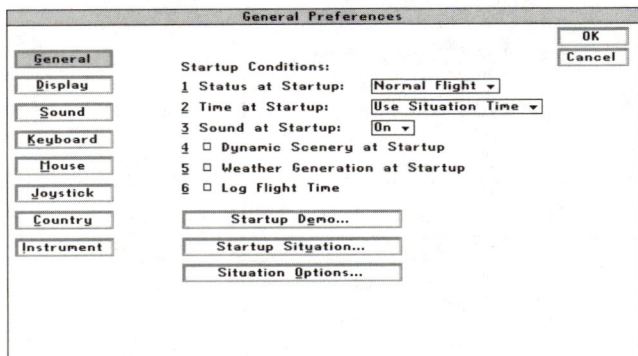

The General Preferences dialog window

Click on the words **Status at Startup:** or press the
1 key. A small menu appears to the right. Select
Demo. Flight. and then click on **OK** or press **Enter**.

The action will ensure that each time we start up
the Flight Simulator, a demonstration will be given.
After a while you will find this unnecessary or even
boring and you can switch it off again. But we shall
now have a look to see how it all works.

Open the **Options** menu and then press **X**. The following window appears:

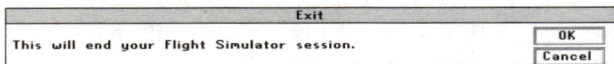

The Exit window

Select **OK** or press **Enter**.

We now return to MS-DOS. To be able to see the demonstration, we have to start up the Flight Simulator again.

Now type: **fs5** and press **Enter**.

The program starts up again but begins this time with a demonstration. The demo lasts for about seven minutes. First you see the Cessna taking off from Meigs Field. Examine the instruments closely and see if you can follow what's going on. The communication line provides information in aircraft terms about what is happening. Don't worry if you cannot follow it yet.

We're flying - even if we're being flown

After roughly three and a half minutes, a different aeroplane appears on the screen. It is a dual or twin engine aircraft. The cockpit is quite different to that of the Cessna. If you have seen enough, press the **Esc** key to stop the demo. Then click on **OK** or press **Enter**.

Are you ready to take off yourself? Yes, why not?

Open the **Options** menu again and select **Preferences**. Now choose **Normal Flight** instead of **Demo Flight** at the **Status at Startup** section (1). Click on **OK** or press **Enter**. Then open the **Options** menu and select the **Reset Situation** option. You now come into the same situation as at the very beginning, on runway 36 of Meigs Field, Chicago.

Some important keys

Before taking to the air, we shall give a summary of several keys which are very important when you are busy with the Flight Simulator.

THE KEYBOARD

the throttle

F1	throttle closed
F2	less fuel
F3	more fuel
F4	fully open

the flaps

F5   flaps up
F6   flaps down a little (10 degrees)
F7   flaps down further (30 degrees)
F8   flaps down as far as possible.

ailerons and rudder

the ← and → cursor keys

elevator

up   ↓
down ↑

brakes (on the ground)

brake   the . key (the dot)
parking brakes   Ctrl-. (Ctrl and the dot together)

You can also perform all these actions using the mouse. We shall remind you how this works. By pressing the **right** mouse button, you can switch back and forward between operating the menus and operating the Flight Simulator itself. If the mouse pointer is shown, you can operate the menus. If you then press the **right** mouse button, the mouse pointer disappears and you can perform the actions listed overleaf. The mouse pointer reappears when you press the right mouse button again.

The actions listed overleaf are only carried out if you cannot see the mouse pointer (does not apply to the flaps).

THE MOUSE

the throttle

hold down the left mouse button and move the mouse forwards for more throttle and backwards for less

ailerons and rudder

move the mouse to the left (for left bank) and right (right bank); do **not** press the mouse button

elevator

move mouse backwards (nose up) and forwards (nose down); do **not** hold down the mouse button

brakes (on the ground)

brake on: move the mouse to the left while holding down the left mouse button.

release brake: move the mouse to the right while holding down the left mouse button.

the flaps

Click here to operate the flaps

As mentioned, we shall generally give the operating instructions from the keyboard. This is more convenient than using the mouse, certainly at the beginning. You can give more accurate commands. If we mention the **joystick**, you can always use the keyboard instead.

| i | **'SHARPER' INSTRUMENTS** |

If you find the instruments to be a little hazy on your screen, you can improve the display. Open the **Options** menu and select **Preferences**. The select **Instrument** from the subsequent dialog window and in the Panel Display section, change the word **Photo-realistic** to **Enhanced Readability**. Then click on **OK** or press **Enter**. This helps greatly, especially with normal VGA cards.

Finally, really taking off

Here we go! In the left-hand corner of the window, you will see the words **PARKING BRAKES**. These have to be released first.

Press the **.** (the dot).

We operate the **throttle** using the function keys F1 to F4. F1 means cut the throttle, F4 means full throttle, F2 means less and F3 means more.

Check if the guiding controls are neutral by looking at the 'rulers' between the artificial horizon and altimeter. If you have not altered any of the settings, the elevator will be roughly two stripes above the middle line.

Open the throttle and go!

Press and hold down the **F3** key.

You will hear that the engine makes more revs.
The small lever in the lower right-hand corner rises.
When it cannot go any higher, release the F3 key.
The aeroplane begins to move over the runway.
You will see the speed indicator increasing.

When the speed indicator reaches **50 knots**, you
can begin slowly pulling the joystick. If you are
using the keyboard, press the ↓. The aeroplane
begins climbing.

When you can no longer see the runway, press the
G.

This raises the landing gear (sometimes called
'undercarriage'). Because the aeroplane now has
less air resistance, it begins to climb more quickly.
Look at your vertical speed indicator. You can now
change the speed of the plane by changing the
position of the nose. If you move the nose down a
little, you will fly more quickly. The vertical climbing
speed then decreases. The position of the nose is
often referred to as the **pitch**.

Climbing at the right speed

Now try using the joystick or the cursor keys to
reach a speed of around 80 knots. You will see that
the vertical climbing speed is approximately 800-
900 feet per minute.

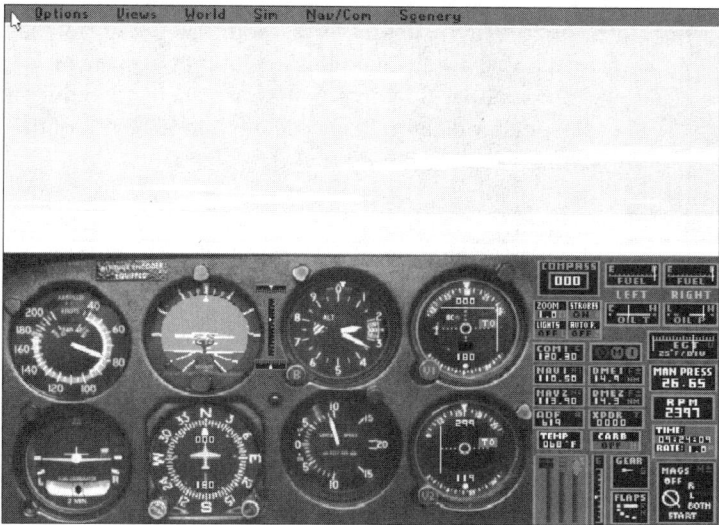

Going up

It is very difficult, initially, to control your speed because you have the feeling that you're 'running after' your airspeed indicator. You feel as if you are constantly busy making corrections. The artificial horizon can help you here.

Look at the artificial horizontal. Try to make sure that the aeroplane symbol remains just above the horizon (the border between the blue and brown areas). Now take a look at the airspeed indicator. If it is more than 80 knots, bring the nose up a little and wait to see if the speed becomes stable.

In this way, you can make small corrections. In the meantime, we are still climbing. If you look out of the cockpit window, you will just be able to see the horizon. If you keep this in mind, you will know that when you are flying in this position at full power, your speed is 80 knots. You don't really need the airspeed indicator. You only need to look out of the window to see how fast you're going.

Initially, everything seems to go at a terrible pace. So many things are happening. But when you have practised a few times (and probably made a few nosedives) you will begin to get the hang of it. Then it doesn't seem so fast.

No more climbing

It's now time to stop climbing. We shall attempt to fly on a steady altitude of **3000** feet.

Just before you reach the required altitude, you can begin to level off the nose of the plane (the pitch). The greater the climbing speed of the plane, the earlier you have to begin this process of levelling off, otherwise you will climb through your required altitude. A good way of remembering how to do this is as follows: if your vertical climbing speed is 500 feet per minute, you should begin levelling off 50 feet before reaching the required altitude. In general thus, you should begin levelling off at a height which is 10% of your vertical climbing speed, simply converted.

If you reach the required altitude and leave the throttle as it is, you will see that the speed begins to increase. The extra power which was used to climb into the air is now transformed into a higher for-

wards speed. The Cessna you are flying is equipped
with a so-called **constant speed propeller**. This
means that a specified number of propeller revolutions (revs) is automatically maintained. Thus, even
if you give less throttle, the propeller revs remain
the same. This is possible because the propeller
blades are adjustable (see the figure below).

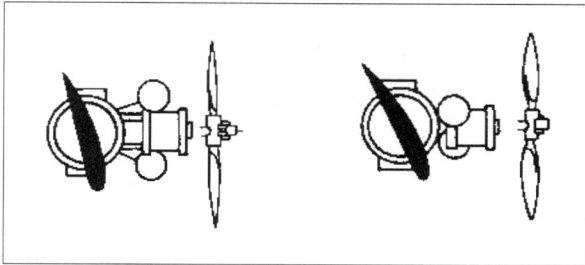

The propeller blades can be adjusted

Regulating the engine power

During the start and the climb, the number of revs
was 2400. This is displayed above the throttle. In
order to find out exactly how much power the
engine has, you need a different instrument. This is
an instrument which displays the so-called **manifold
pressure**.

If you have a Super VGA card, you will be able to
see the dial quite clearly at the extreme right-hand
side of the dashboard, above the revolutions dial.

The right-hand side of the dashboard if you have a Super VGA graphic card.

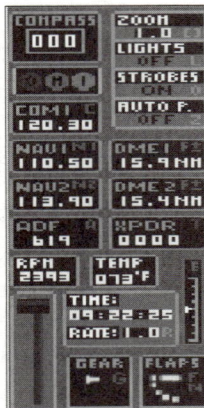

The right-hand side of the dashboard if you have a VGA or EGA graphic card.

If you have a normal VGA card or an EGA card, you can keep on looking but you will not be able to find this instrument. To prevent the screen becoming too full when these cards are used, some instruments are concealed. You can nevertheless show them on the screen by pressing the **Tab** key. Try it out.

The right-hand side of the dashboard with VGA/EGA cards, after Tab has been pressed

All the **engine instruments** are now shown at the right-hand side of the screen. The two at the top are the fuel meters. Both tanks are completely full. Under these are the meters for **oil temperature** and **oil pressure**. When flying, the needles should be in the green area. Under these, there is a meter showing **EGT**. EGT is an abbreviation of **exhaust gas temperature**. Under this is the instrument we were looking for in the first place, the **manifold pressure** meter. If you are flying at 3000 feet at full power, it should show almost 26. If you ease the throttle back a bit by pressing F2, you will see that the manifold pressure is reduced although the number of revs (2400) remains the same. Your speed will increase to around 120 knots. The two levers (buttons) next to the throttle are the **propeller control** (blue) and the **mixture control** (red). You can operate these separately, but they are working automatically at the moment.

The same advice applies to flying straight and level as to climbing. If you look out of the cockpit and note the position of the nose of the aircraft in relation to the horizon, you can remember that this position corresponds to a manifold pressure of **23** and a speed of roughly **145** knots.

Climbing higher

So, getting the hang of it? Now we shall climb to 5000 feet. Open the throttle by pressing F3 several times (or F4 once). Bring the nose into the same position as during the initial climb. When you get to 5000 feet, reduce the throttle so that the manifold pressure is reduced to 23. Perhaps you'll find it all a bit difficult at first, but practice makes perfect as we all know.

Going down again

It is now time to practise descending. This can be done in two ways. The first way is to close the throttle. This is done by pressing **F2** several times or by pressing **F1** once. Also press the **H** key once. This switches on the **carburetor heating system**. This allows warm air into the carburetor so that it will not freeze shut if you are flying in cold, damp conditions. This is necessary because the motor cools down. You will notice that the nose of the aircraft now tends to point downwards. You can regulate your speed by adjusting the pitch. Try to keep a steady speed of 100 knots. If the speed becomes too great, raise the nose a little; if the speed is reduced too much, lower the nose again. When the speed is stabilised at around 100 knots, you will descend at a rate of around 700-800 feet per minute.

We shall level off at a height of 3000 feet. In that case, just as with climbing, take 10% of your vertical speed (this is then 70-80 feet) and begin levelling off at that point (thus at 3070 feet). This is done by increasing the throttle to a manifold pressure of 23. Press the **H** key once more. This switches the carburetor heating system off again. You can see whether or not the carburetor heating system is on or off by looking at the small panel under the RPM (revs per minute) indicator. This is to the left of the RPM indicator with SVGA screens and to the right with VGA/EGA screens. It shows **CARB H** and On or OFF will be shown underneath. Because you increase your power, the nose rises a little. You can make small corrections by means of the control yoke or joystick in order to keep on flying at an altitude of 3000 feet.

ℹ️   **IS STEERING DIFFICULT?**

A real aeroplane also reacts very sensitively to movements of the
joystick or control yoke. But if you really find that the steering
devices are too sensitive, you can make changes.

Open the **Options** menu and select **Preferences**. If you are
steering using the cursor keys, choose **Keyboard**. Three lines
appear, each with a scale showing 1 to 8.

```
┌──────────────────────────────────────────────────────────────┐
│                     Keyboard Preferences                        │
│            The higher the sensitivity setting,      ┌──────┐   │
│            the more exacting and difficult          │  OK  │   │
│  General   it is to control the aircraft.           └──────┘   │
│                                                     ┌──────┐   │
│  Display                                            │Cancel│   │
│                                                     └──────┘   │
│  Sound                                                         │
│                                              Low         High  │
│  Keyboard  Aileron Sensitivity:             1 2 3 4 5 6 7 8   │
│                                                  ▲             │
│  Mouse                                       Low         High  │
│            Elevator Sensitivity:            1 2 3 4 5 6 7 8   │
│  Joystick                                           ▲         │
│                                              Low         High  │
│  Country   Rudder Sensitivity:              1 2 3 4 5 6 7 8   │
│                                                     ▲         │
│  Instrument                                                    │
│                                                                │
│  If you check the box below, Flight Simulator will load the    │
│  sensitivities you saved with the situation and not the ones   │
│  above.                                                        │
│  □ Load Sensitivities Saved with Situation                     │
└──────────────────────────────────────────────────────────────┘
```

The normal setting is roughly in the middle, at 4.5. If you have a
mouse, you can move the small triangle to the required position
by clicking on it and dragging it to the left or right. If you do not
have a mouse, press the **Alt** key and then the **A**. The top line
becomes red. Then type a 3. Do the same with **Alt-E** and **Alt-R** to
reduce the sensitivity of the elevator and the rudder. If you are
flying using a joystick, click on the **Joystick** button. Making the
settings then takes place in the same way.

When you have clicked on **OK** or pressed **Enter**, you will notice
that your plane reacts less nervously to your instructions. Try different settings to find out the one that is best for you.

A different way of going down

The second way of going down is a bit more even. Instead of closing the throttle completely, you cut down the throttle just a little so that the rate of descent is not so great. This is also better for the engine because it does not cool down so quickly. The aviation term is 'cruise descent'. If you have not made any further changes, you will still be flying at 3000 feet. We shall now descend to 2000 feet. Close down the throttle until the manifold pressure becomes 17 and use the mouse, joystick or cursor keys to ensure that the pitch produces roughly 140 knots. You will see that you descend at a rate of approximately 500 feet per minute.

Going down

You should also notice that the aeroplane now reacts more quickly to steering commands because the speed has increased. When you are flying at 2000 feet, adjust the throttle so that the manifold pressure becomes 23 again.

We have now learned quite a lot. It may be a bit of a rough ride at the moment, but every beginning is difficult. Persevere.

Round the bend

Up until now we have only flown in one direction. It is now time to practise turning, otherwise we shall never return to the airport. If everything has gone as it should, we are still flying northwards. The heading indicator shows **000**.

In order to make a good turn, you should use both the ailerons and the rudder. These are normally linked in the Flight Simulator. Thus, if you turn the control yoke to the left, the ailerons are adjusted correspondingly (the left aileron is raised and the right aileron is lowered) and the rudder is also moved so that the aircraft will turn to the left.

When you have gained a little more experience with the Flight Simulator, or if you want to try out special manoeuvres, you can break this link. We shall deal with this further on in the book.

Look carefully and then turn left

We shall first make a **left turn** of **360** degrees in such a way that we end up going in the same direction. First we have to take a quick look left to see that there is no other air traffic in our way. In the Flight Simulator, you can look left by pressing the **Scroll Lock** key and then the ← key on the numeric keypad at the right-hand side of the keyboard. Try it.

Looking left

You see the underside of the wing and the wing support or wing strut. To look forwards again, press the **Scroll Lock** key again and then the ↑ key.

Okay. We are now looking forwards again. Now move the control yoke to the left so that the aero-

plane banks roughly **30** degrees. You can see this
on the artificial horizon. The first two short stripes
indicate an inclination of 10 and 20 degrees respectively. The third, longer, stripe indicates a bank
(inclination) of 30 degrees.

The pilot comes from a banking family

You will notice that the aircraft begins to descend.
This is due to the fact that a part of the wing lift is
now being used to make the turn. Therefore, when
turning, you have to adjust the control yoke or joystick so that you keep the same altitude. You notice
that you have to keep track of many things at once:
the artificial horizon, to make sure that the bank
remains 30 degrees; the altimeter to make sure you
keep to 2000 feet; and your heading indicator, so
that you can come out of the turn and continue in a
northerly direction.

And straight forwards again

When the heading indicator displays **015**, you should begin to move the control yoke or joystick slowly to the right. We call this **rolling out** of the turn. If you execute this properly, the wings should be exactly parallel to the horizon when your heading indicator shows 000 degrees, thus due north. A good aid to memory is: **begin rolling out when the distance to the required course is equal to half of the number of degrees of inclination**. Thus, if you have a banking attitude of 30 degrees, you should start rolling out when you reach 15 degrees before the required direction. If you make a steep turn of 60 degrees, start rolling out 30 degrees before you reach the required direction. If you're not successful the first time (that would be a miracle), make small adjustments until your heading indicator displays 000 degrees.

A turn to the right is of course just the reverse of a turn to the left. Remember to glance quickly to the right before making the turn. Press **Scroll Lock** and then the → key. Then press the **Scroll Lock** key and then ↑ so that you are looking forward again. Now move the joystick or control yoke slowly to the right and raise the nose a little to maintain altitude.

Back to Chicago

In the meantime, we have travelled quite a distance from the airport from which we took off. We shall now attempt to make a turn to the left and roll out of it on a course of **180** degrees. Thus, we want to go southwards again.

Using the map

Turn to the left. You will see Lake Michigan in the
distance. After a while Chicago itself will come into
view. If you cannot find the Lake, press the **Num
Lock** key. A map appears on the screen.

*It's a beautiful view. And a coconut to the man who
invented the map!*

NOTE: If you are operating the aircraft by means of
the cursor keys, you will have to press the **Num
Lock** key once again. If you don't do that, the cursor
keys are blocked.

You can use the **+** and **-** keys on the 'normal' part of the keyboard to increase or decrease the scale of the map. If you want to remove the map from the screen, press the **Num Lock** key twice in rapid succession. Chicago appears when you simply follow the west shore of the lake. When you see the airport, you can descend to an altitude of 1600 feet. That is roughly 1000 feet above the ground (Chicago lies at an altitude of almost 600 feet above sea level). We shorten this to '1000 **AGL**' (above ground level).

Help! I have to land!

What should we do now? We have to land of course, but we haven't learned how. It might be an idea to draw up a will. Fortunately, we can get some help. There is an instructor who can assist us.

Press the **X** key or open the *Options* menu and select **Land Me**. An instructor takes control of the plane and will land it for you. You don't need to pay very close attention to how this is done - it often takes place rather roughly. But the plane is landed in one piece even if the passengers are all shook up.

Whew, almost down safely

So, here we are on the ground again. You can take
control again.

Looking for a parking place

We have to leave the runway; it's not a garage.
Open the throttle a little and taxi down the runway.
If you go too fast, you can brake by pressing the **.**
(the dot). If you want to move a bit quicker, open
the throttle. The best way to see where you are is to
display the area map on the screen. This is done by
pressing the **Num Lock** key. Take one of the turn-
ings to the left. When you have left the runway,
press **F5** to raise the flaps. You can also switch the
strobe lights off by pressing the **O** (not the zero).

Then the traffic on the ground will not be disturbed by these lights.

Taxi down the yellow line. The Air Traffic Control tower is on the left. When you taxi a little further, you will come to an area marked in yellow showing an F. This is easy to recognise on the map. Move gently into this parking area. When you park here, the fuel tanks are refilled. Apply the parking brakes by pressing **Ctrl-.**.

Switching off the engine

Ensure that you have a good view of the instruments. If you have a Super VGA card, they will be displayed automatically, but otherwise you will have to press the **Tab** key. The contact switch is in the lower right-hand corner.
In this case, it is referred to as the **Magnetos switch**. The magnetos supply current to the spark plugs.

The Magnetos switch

The aeroplane has a dual contact system (for the left and right magnetos). The switch is currently set to 'BOTH'. Now switch it to off by clicking with the mouse or by pressing the **M** key and then the **-** key three times. The switch moves to OFF.

So, that was our first flight. You can now leave the program by opening the **Options** menu and selecting **Exit**. If, during the installation, you chose to keep a logbook, it will be displayed when you click on OK in the small window which now appears. The Flight Simulator automatically keeps track of your flying time. You can enter information yourself on the blank line, such as 'The first flight using the Flight Simulator'. Then click on **OK** or press **Enter** and you quit the program.

---

i   **USING CTRL-BREAK TO STOP MORE QUICKLY**

You can stop the program more quickly by pressing **Ctrl-Break**. You can do that at any given moment.

You may have had some difficulty with some aspects of the program, but remember that a real plane is easier to operate than the Flight Simulator. In addition, you see and feel more in a real plane so that you can get an idea of what is going on more quickly. But if you keep on practising, you will soon get the hang of things.

We have now dealt with the so-called **Four fundamentals of flight**: straight and level flight, turning, climbing and descending. All other manoeuvres are combinations of these basic actions. As you see, flying is not as difficult as you may have imagined.

3   The built-in instructor

In the previous chapter, we discussed how to start, climb, turn and descend. The Flight Simulator also supplies a whole series of flying lessons. You can activate these by opening the **Options** menu and selecting **Flight Instruction**.

There are 25 lessons, subdivided into three categories. The first of these is the **Basic** category. This contains 10 lessons which deal with the first steps in flying. This contains, thus, many of the things you learned in the previous chapter. In the second category, **Advanced**, there are 8 lessons dealing with more advanced techniques. The last category, **Aerobatic**, teaches you how to approach figure flying. But we have to learn a lot before we reach that stage.

As mentioned, we have already discussed many of the things in the **Basic** category. Let's look at the first lesson in the program. You will see that lesson 1 is selected when you choose the **Flying Instruction** option. Click on **OK** or press **Enter**. The first lesson dealing with taxiing begins. The Instructor Control bar is shown, indicating that the Instructor will demonstrate the manoeuvres first. The middle of the runway is shown by a yellow line.

Taxi!

The instructor now taxis along the taxiway which is parallel to the runway, and stops there. Then you can try it out yourself: (**STARTING STUDENT MODE**). At the end of each lesson, the program makes some comments about your style. Don't get agitated. If you work through the entire basic instruction program, you will become a reasonable pilot.

If you examine the dialog window which appears when you select **Flying Instruction**, you will see the option **Lessons in Sequence** at the bottom of the dialog window. If you activate this option, all the lessons are given, one by one, in sequence: when you have finished the first lesson, you move on automatically to the second, and so on. If the instructor demonstrates something which you think you can master, press the **Esc** key. From that moment onwards, you have control over the plane. Accordingly, you do not always have to wait until the instructor has finished before you can get to work yourself. You can also simply begin yourself by activating the **Student Control** option at the bottom of the dialog window.

---

i ## ZOOMING IN AND OUT

If you are looking out the window, you can enlarge the object which you are looking at. This is done by pressing the equals sign (**=**). Press the minus sign (**-**) to zoom out again. If you hold down the **Shift** key while zooming in or out, the zooming will take place in smaller steps. This also works in the same way with the small map which you can display on the screen. The amount of Zoom is shown on the instrument panel at the right-hand side of your screen. With normal vision, this is **1.0**.

4 Practising landing

You have now become acquainted with the aircraft.
We can therefore begin with the most difficult part
of flying. Taking off takes place almost automatically, but getting the plane down on the ground in one
piece demands much more effort. The **Land Me**
function helped us in the previous chapter, and you
have probably made a couple of attempts on your
own. You will realise that the ground is quite hard
and that gravity is merciless.

Flying on to another airport

We shall first fly on to an airport with a long runway
so that there is plenty of room to practise. Open the
World menu and select the second option,
Airports. The following menu appears:

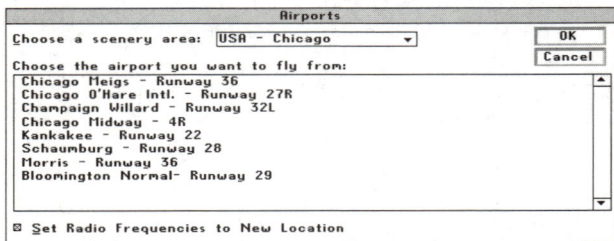

The Airports menu

Click on the small triangle behind **USA - Chicago** or
press **C**. A choice is presented of five different areas
in the USA and two in Europe. Select **USA Seattle**.
A list of airports in that area is then displayed. The
second line contains the option, **Boeing Field -**

Runway 31L. Select this option and click on **OK** or press **Enter**. We are magically transported to runway 31L of Boeing Field in Seattle. Test flights with the large Boeings are carried out here. If the runway is large enough for these aircraft, it should be large enough for us.

No Boeing in sight - fortunately!

By the way, **31L** means that the runway lies in the direction of **310 degrees** (rounded off) and that it is the **left** runway of the two available.

The traffic pattern

Large airports with Air Traffic Control instruct you how to come in and land. They provide information

about altitudes and/or determine a certain course
you have to follow to land on a certain runway.
They also make sure that you do not come too
close to other aircraft. Smaller airports do not provide this service and you have to do it all yourself.
Of course, you cannot just arrive at an airport and
make yourself at home. Other planes in the neighbourhood do not know what to expect and you
also do not know what their plans are. Accordingly,
everybody has to fly in a specific **traffic pattern**.
This resembles the figure shown below.

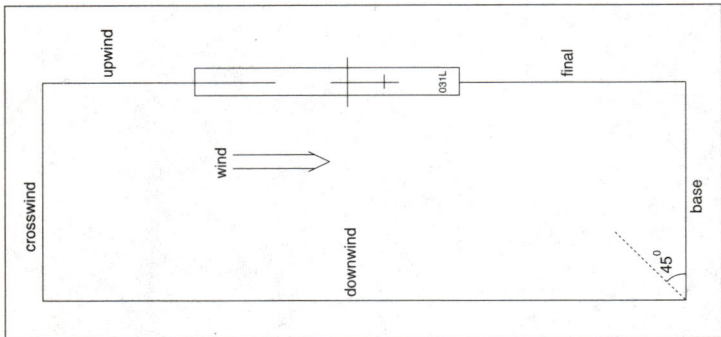

The traffic pattern

The runway is shown in the figure. Normally, you
begin into the wind as much as possible. The first
part of the pattern is thus called the **upwind leg**.
The second part turns to the left and is called the
crosswind leg because the wind comes from the
side. If there is no special information on the map of
the area, this means that the traffic pattern is a left-
hand pattern; in other words, you turn to the left at
each turning point in the circuit. Some airports have
right-hand traffic patterns so that all turns in the cir-

cuit are made to the right. When you come to the **downwind leg**, you are flying parallel to the runway with the wind at your back. The following leg is the **base leg**, and the last stage, the stage in which the pilot lines up to actually land, is called the **final leg**.

Here we go!

Shall we give it a try? We shall take a couple of safety precautions first. Open the **Sim** menu and select **Crash Detection**. The Crash Detection dialog window appears.

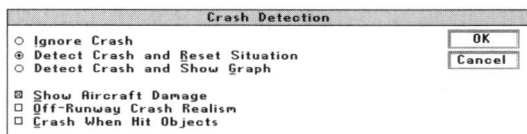

```
┌──────────────────────── Crash Detection ────────────────────────┐
│ ○ Ignore Crash                                    ┌─────────┐    │
│ ⊙ Detect Crash and Reset Situation                │   OK    │    │
│ ○ Detect Crash and Show Graph                     ├─────────┤    │
│                                                   │ Cancel  │    │
│ ☒ Show Aircraft Damage                            └─────────┘    │
│ ☐ Off-Runway Crash Realism                                       │
│ ☐ Crash When Hit Objects                                         │
└──────────────────────────────────────────────────────────────────┘
```

The Crash Detection dialog window

There is probably a dot in the **Detect Crash and Reset Situation** option button. This means that after a crash, the Flight Simulator begins all over again at the original situation. In this case, it will be Meigs Field in Chicago. To prevent having to move to Boeing Field again via the menu options, we shall now select the **Ignore Crash** option. If you now crash, nothing will happen.

OK. We are now at the beginning of runway 31L at Boeing Field. The Air Traffic Control tower is shown a little to the left and the highrise buildings of Seattle are visible in the distance. Even the 'Space Needle' can be seen. Imagine that the Air Traffic

Control has just transmitted 'Cleared for Take-Off'.
We can release the parking brakes and we can
open the throttle for take off. Keep an eye on the
engine instruments. Oil pressure and temperature
are fine, the manifold pressure increases to roughly
29 and the revs show 2400. The speed of the aircraft increases. When you reach approximately 50
or 55 knots, you can begin to rise by pulling back
the joystick (or press the ↓ key 3 or 4 times). The aircraft begins to lift. Keep the wings horizontal. When
you can no longer see the runway, raise the landing
gear by pressing **G**. Now regulate your speed by
adjusting the pitch. Try to maintain a constant
speed of 80 knots. Climb to an altitude of 1000
feet. That is the altitude of the **traffic pattern** at
most airports. In this case, this always refers to the
altitude **above ground level**. Since Seattle airport is
roughly at sea level, it makes little difference here,
but for example, O'Hare Airport in Chicago lies at
an altitude of 667 feet, so that the traffic pattern
there is at an altitude of 1700 feet above sea level.

Going to the crosswind and downwind legs

When you have become used to flying with the
Flight Simulator, you can turn into the crosswind at
an altitude of 400 feet. But we shall climb to 1000
feet just to be sure. Then reduce the throttle so that
the manifold pressure becomes 17 with a speed of
about 100 knots. Check that the landing gear and
the flaps have been brought in. Then we can turn
into the crosswind. When we started, our course
was 310 degrees. The crosswind leg is at a right-
angle to this so that our course should become **220**

degrees. We shall maintain this course for about half a minute. Then we turn again to the left, to a course parallel to the original one but in the opposite direction. This means a course of **130** degrees.

Preparing to land

Look to the left now and again to see if you can see the runway. Remember how that was done? That's right, first press **Scroll Lock** and then press ← on the numeric keypad. When you get to a point opposite the beginning of the runway, switch on the carburetor heating by pressing **H** and lower the landing gear by pressing **G**. This increases the air resistance and the plane will begin to lose height. Now position the flaps at 10 degrees by pressing the **F6** key, and maintain a speed of 90 knots. When the beginning of the runway is behind you (at an angle of roughly 45 degrees), turn into the **base leg**.

You can look diagonally behind you by pressing **Scroll Lock** and then **1**. The new course will have become 040 degrees. Now try to maintain an airspeed of 80 knots. Look now and again diagonally to the left by pressing **Scroll Lock** and then **7**. Then you can estimate when you have to turn into the **final leg** prior to landing.

In the final leg

Once you get to the final leg, position the flaps at 30 degrees by pressing **F7**. Maintain a speed of 70 knots. You can get some assistance from the lights at the left hand side of the runway. If you see two white lights, this means you are too high; if you see two red lights, you are too low. If the furthest light is red and the nearest one is white, you are at exactly the right altitude.

In the end there was light

The lights alongside the runway are referred to as **VASI**. This is short for **Visual Approach Slope Indicator**. Accordingly, they indicate whether or not you are approaching the runway at the right angle. There is also another indicator to help you assess the necessary height. You need 300 feet for every mile from the runway. Therefore, if you are 5 miles from the runway and you are at a height of 1500 feet, you are on the right glide slope. It is not very easy to estimate this on the Flight Simulator, thus it is not a very clear indicator, but when we fly with the aid of navigation beacons later we can make use of it. There are beacons at many airports and your instruments indicate your distance from the runway.

Landing!

But let us not lose concentration. We are on the final leg, hopefully at the right altitude and speed. If this is not the case, make small corrections until you're on the right approach. The runway is coming closer and we are descending with a speed of 500 feet per minute. If we continue like this, we shall not have a very pleasant encounter with the runway.

We shall reduce our speed of descent.

Almost there

When we are just above the runway - the exact moment is a question of practice - we close the throttle and lift the nose of the plane so that the main landing gear hits the ground first. When the speed is further reduced, the nosewheel is lowered automatically because the low speed means that there is almost no air current along the horizontal stabiliser and the elevator. Then you can brake by pressing the **.** key (the dot), and turn off the runway. When you have left the runway, raise the flaps and taxi back to the beginning of the runway to practise taking off and landing a few times. It will take plenty of practice to be able to make faultless landings. When you have mastered that to a reasonable extent, proceed to the next exercises.

Taking off and landing with crosswind

In our first exercises in taking off and landing, we began under ideal conditions. We had a long runway and there was no wind, or the wind blew along the length of the runway. In real flight, that is seldom the case. Planners have a good look at the direction of the prevailing winds when an airport is being built, but even then, in practice, the wind does not always blow along the runway.

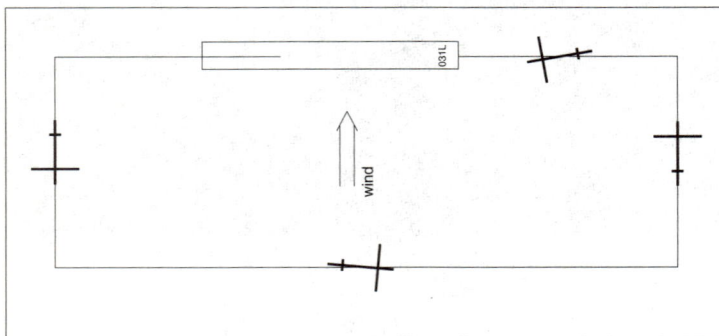

Necessary corrections due to crosswind in the traffic pattern

Examine the figure above. You will notice that you will have to make corrections to compensate for the wind if you want to fly in a rectangle. Up until now, we have flown with the ailerons and the rudder linked to one another. When you turn to the left, the rudder is turned to the left and at the same time, the left aileron is raised and the right aileron lowered. We shall now change this situation.

Examining the aircraft from the side

We shall demonstrate how this works by looking at
our own Cessna from the side. This is easily done.
We shall presume that the aeroplane is standing on
the runway at Boeing Field. Press the **S** key twice
and then the **+** key once.

Our Cessna from the side

Now move the joystick back and forth (or press the
← and → keys). If you look closely, you will see the
rudder and the ailerons move.

Separating the rudder and the ailerons

Now open the **Sim** menu. The **Auto Coordination** option is shown on the fifth line, with a tick mark in front of it which indicates that this option is active. Select this option. This removes the tick mark and thus the Auto Coordination is switched off. Then you can operate the ailerons and the rudder separately. The ailerons are still operated by means of the joystick (or the ← and → keys) and the rudder is now operated by means of the **0** and the **Enter** keys on the numeric keypad. Try it out and look at the screen. You will feel that quite a bit of coordination is required.

We shall return to our normal view by pressing the **S** key again.

Releasing wind

Prior to practising, we shall change the speed and direction of the wind. Open the **World** menu and select **Weather**. You can make all sorts of specifications in the subsequent dialog box.

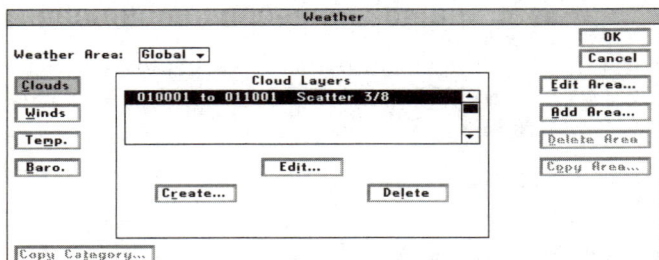

If only we had this menu in real life...

We shall change the wind via the second button at
the left of the window. Click on it using the mouse
or press the letter **W** (the underlined letter). We
want to have the wind blow across the runway at
an angle of 90 degrees. Since we are still on runway
31L at Boeing Field, we shall specify that the wind
should be blowing at 240 degrees at a speed of 10
knots. The wind is then a direct crosswind. This is
done by activating the Create button (click on it or
press **R**). Another dialog window appears.

```
┌───────────────────────────────────────────────────┐
│                 Create Wind Layer                  │
│ ⊕ Wind Aloft - MSL, True               ┌────OK────┐│
│ ○ Surface Wind - AGL, Magnetic         │  Cancel  ││
│                                        └──────────┘│
│ Type:            [Steady ▾]                        │
│ Base (ft MSL):   [001499]                          │
│ Tops (ft MSL):   [002499]                          │
│ Speed (kts):     [000]                             │
│ Direction (True): [000]                            │
│                      Light         Heavy           │
│ Turbulence:        1 2  3  4  5  6  7 8            │
│                    ▲                               │
└───────────────────────────────────────────────────┘
```

The Create Wind Layer menu

At **Base**, the lower limit of the wind, specify **0** and
confirm this by pressing **Enter**. The **0** changes into
00000**3** since that is the altitude of the airport. At
Tops, the upper limit of the wind, specify **5000** for
instance. At the next line, **Speed**, enter the required
speed. In our example, that is **10**. Then specify the
Direction. That is **240**. You can determine that
there should be some turbulence if you wish. We
prefer not to. Finally, click on **OK** or press **Enter**.
You will see that the wind has changed to fit our
specifications. Click on **OK** again or press **Enter**.

Let's give it a try

In the mood? Release the parking brakes and open the throttle gently. The wind, coming from the left, begins to get a hold of the tail which begins to turn like a weather vane, pushing the nose of the plane round to face the wind. But, of course, we want the nose of the plane to continue following the direction of the runway, so you have to turn the rudder a little to the right (by pressing **Enter** on the numeric keypad). The wind coming from the left also has the tendency to blow the wings to the right. You have to turn the ailerons a little to the left to keep the wings on course. Thus, you see that you have to turn the ailerons and the rudder in different directions to keep the plane going in a straight line. This is the reason why we had to switch off the Auto Coordination function. We refer to this style of steering as **slipping**.

It works a bit different in the air

When you are in the air, you have to fly in a coordinated manner. If you remain flying with 'crossed' steering, you will create a lot of extra air resistance. But you should not activate the Auto Coordination function again because you will shortly have to apply these quite differently. Therefore, in the air, you should operate the ailerons and the rudder to conform to one another.

If you are flying on a course of 310 degrees, you will notice that you will slowly drift off to the right. If you want to continue flying in a rectangle in relation to the ground, you will have to compensate by steering a little to the left. Therefore, choose a course of 300 degrees instead of 310. When you are on the crosswind leg, the wind is full in your face so you don't have to make any compensation there. The speed is reduced, in relation to the ground, because you are flying directly into the wind. For this reason, you will have to fly for a bit longer instead of the previous 30 seconds before turning into the downwind leg. You will have to compensate for the win again on this leg; this time the wind is coming from the right. Fly several degrees to the right instead of exactly 130 degrees.

Slipping again when landing

When you get to the final leg, you will have to steer a little to the left to compensate for the wind from that direction. Nevertheless, the aeroplane has to land in the direction of the runway, not at a diagonal. Accordingly, we shall slip through the last stage of the flight. Use the ailerons to turn the wing a little to the left and, at the same time, turn the rudder a little to the right to line up the body of the aircraft with the runway.

If you carry out this manoeuvre properly, the left wheel will touch down first. Then drop the wing a little to the right so that the right wheel makes contact. Then drop the nosewheel. If it is too difficult with a wind speed of 10 knots, practise with less wind, increasing it bit by bit.

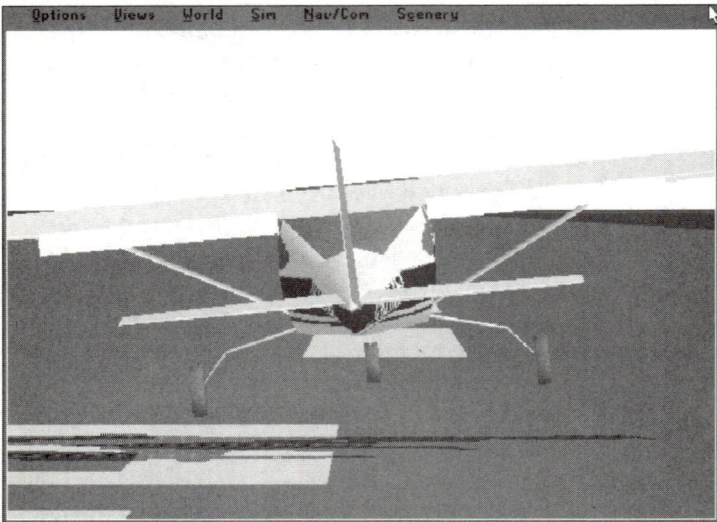

The left wheel touches down first

We're off to Austria

Of course, small aeroplanes do not always take off from and land on large asphalted runways. They are perfectly suited to going to small airports with short runways which might even have obstacles in front or at the end of them. They might not even be asphalted at all. In such cases, you have to make a so-called **shortfield take off** or a **softfield take off** and the corresponding landing.

For this adventure, we shall whiz ourselves off to **Zell am See** in Austria. We have already seen that we can go to a large number of airports via the **World** menu. But if you select **Germany-Munich**

from the **Airports** menu option, which is the area
which includes Zell am See (for the Flight
Simulator), you will see that this airport is not shown
in the list. So, how can we get there? If you return to
the **World** menu, you will see that the third line provides the **Set Exact Location** option. Select it.

Specifying the coordinates

By specifying coordinates in the menu that appears
on your screen, you can be placed at that specified
position. We shall now specify that we wish to go to
a position with a latitude of **N047 17 31.4877** and a
Longitude of **E012 47 10.0877**. Behind
North/South Lat., type these coordinates when you
have activated the line by pressing **N** or by clicking
using the mouse. (Did you notice that the program
changes the '77' to '76'?) Press **Enter** to confirm
and type the other coordinates behind **East/West
Lon.** when you have activated that block. Make
sure that there is a space behind N047 and behind
17, and also behind E012 and 47. We must now
type an **altitude** of **2473** feet, which is the altitude
of the airport in Zell am See. Finally, we have to
type the **Heading**: this is **50**. The last two blocks are
activated in the familiar manner (clicking or using **A**
and **H**).

```
                              Set Exact Location
 Set Location of:  Aircraft ▼                                    ┌──────┐
 ⊙ Set Location with Latitude/Longitude                          │  OK  │
    North/South Lat.:   N047° 17' 31.4876"        N047° 17' 31.4876"  └──────┘
    East/West Lon.:     E012° 47' 10.0876"        E012° 47' 10.0876"  ┌──────┐
                                                                 │Cancel│
 ○ Set Location with X/Z coordinates                             └──────┘
    North:              16639.5759                16639.5759
    East:               17203.8377                17203.8377
    Region:             Europe ▼
 Altitude (ft):         +002473                   +002473
 Heading (deg magnetic): 050.00                   050.00
 Note: To cancel changes and reset to the original
 latitude/longitude or X/Z coordinates, choose the Cancel
 button.
 ┌──────────────────────────────────────────────┐
 │ Set Tower View (from Aircraft Location)       │
 └──────────────────────────────────────────────┘
```

An extremely handy dialog window

When you have filled in everything properly, click
on **OK** or press **Enter**.

Then - although it might take a few moments - you
will find yourself at the beginning of runway 5 at
Zell am See airport. The coordinates of the current
position are shown at the top of the screen. After a
short while, they disappear. If they don't go of their
own free will, press **Y** to remove them.

Taking off from Zell am See

You will notice immediately that this runway is
much narrower than those we have used up until
now (look at the map by pressing Num Lock).
Because the runway is also shorter, we shall take off
with the **flaps lowered** by 10 degrees. In this position, the wing produces more lift even if the plane is
travelling with less speed, enabling us to take off
sooner. Press **F6** and examine if your flaps have
moved to the correct position. You can check this

on the small flap position indicator in the lower
right-hand corner, but you can also look out the
window to the left or right by pressing **Scroll Lock**
and ← or →. You will see that the flaps are extended a little.

The flaps are extended

Keep the parking brakes on and begin to rev up.
Check that the engine has enough power and then
release the brakes. Lift the nose from the ground
when you reach a speed of 50 knots. You now
begin climbing with a speed of around 60 knots.
Keep climbing until you reach a safe altitude of 200
feet so that you will clear any obstacles at the end
of the runway. Then accelerate to the normal climbing speed and raise the flaps again (with **F5**). The
rest of the traffic pattern is as normal, except on the

final leg. Up until now we have had the flaps at an angle of 30 degrees on the final leg. If you press **F8**, the flaps are placed at an angle of **40 degrees**. This produces much more air resistance. The angle of approach becomes steeper, allowing you to make a better estimate of where you will touch down. This is very important on a short runway of course, and if there are obstacles at the beginning of the runway, you can avoid them and still make the most efficient use of the remaining runway. This is shown on the figure below. Line A shows the angle of flight with the flaps at 30 degrees and line B shows the angle with the flaps at 40 degrees. You will notice that with line B the angle of descent is much steeper. This exercise is not easy, particularly due to the fact that there are no VASI lights along the runway to indicate whether you are flying at the proper altitude or not. But it is good fun, don't you think?

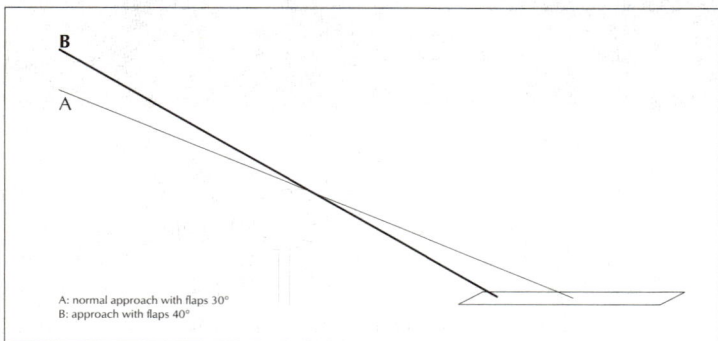

A: normal approach with flaps 30°
B: approach with flaps 40°

The difference between the flaps at 30 and at 40 degrees

5   Navigating

Up until now, we have always landed at the same airport as that from which we took off. But of course, one of the marvellous things about flying is that you can travel enormous distances in a short time. How do you find your way from one airport to the other? There are various ways of doing this.

Pilotage and dead reckoning

The first method we shall deal with is called **pilotage**. You draw a line on a map from one airport to another and you look for prominent features on the way, such as highways, railway lines, lakes, rivers, hills and so on. They help guide you to your destination. It may seem a bit old-fashioned, but it is an interesting way of navigation and it works fine, except when you have to fly over monotonous, featureless ground such as desert or forest, or sea.

The second method of navigation is called **dead reckoning**. Again you draw a line on the map and you calculate the course from one airport to the other. You make corrections for the wind and you work out the length of time you have to hold a particular course in order to arrive at the required point. Unfortunately, because the Flight Simulator provides no useful maps, we cannot make much use of this method.

Dead reckoning?

Radio

We can make use of the third form of navigation, namely navigation using **radio beacons**. The Flight Simulator provides various radios which can receive navigation signals so that we can determine our position.

The VORs

There are two dials to the right of the flying instruments.

These are the so-called **VORs**. This is an abbreviation of **VHF Omnidirectional Range**. This means that this type of beacon sends out a radio signal in all directions; you can receive this signal and determine your position.

The VORs

The ADF

Another kind of navigation radio is the **ADF**, the **Automatic Direction Finder**. This is very easy to use, but it is less precise than the VOR. To display the ADF on the screen, you have to open the **Nav/Com** menu. This is an abbreviation for 'navigation and communication'. The **ADF** option is shown on the bottom line. Select this option.

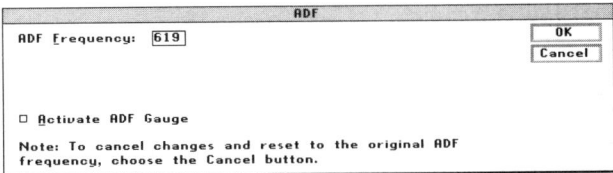

The ADF menu

You can alter the radio frequency in this menu. You can also do this directly on the instrument panel. You will also see the **Activate ADF Gauge** option. If you select this option, the bottom VOR becomes an ADF. In a real plane, both are shown simultaneously

of course, but there is much less space on the
instrument panel in the Flight Simulator so you have
to apply this kind of substitution. Now click on **OK**
or press **Enter** and the new instrument is shown
under the first VOR. This new instrument has a needle and 360 degrees, much like a compass.

The bottom VOR has become an ADF

If you now tune into the frequency of a radio beacon in the neighbourhood, the needle will then
point to the beacon. The beacons which you can
receive on your ADF radio are called **NDBs**. This is
an abbreviation of **non-directional beacon**.

Resuming, the receiver in the plane is an ADF and
the beacons you can receive are NDBs.

Now you only have to fly in the direction indicated
by the needle. If the needle points straight forwards,
you are flying directly towards the beacon. If the
needle points 40 degrees to the left, turn the nose
40 degrees to the left so that the needle points
straight forwards - you are then flying directly
towards the beacon. We shall make a short flight
using the ADF.

The NDB symbol

The figure above shows the NDB symbol. You can also find it on the maps at the back of the Flight Simulator manual (Appendix B). The radio frequency is also given so that you can tune your ADF radio in to the beacon. Note that on the maps the NDB symbols are shown without compass indicator and Morse code.

From St. Johann to Innsbruck

We shall take off from the St. Johann airport in Austria and fly to Innsbruck. The *Pilot's Handbook* (page 219) of the Flight Simulator shows a map with both these airports. A simplified version is shown overleaf.

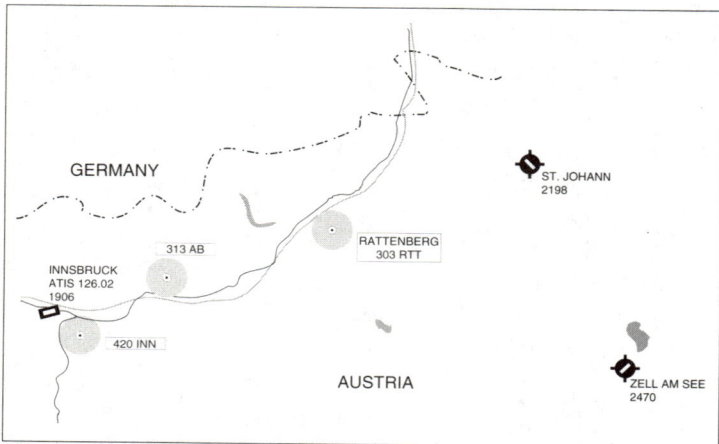

Open the **World** menu and select **Set Exact
Location**. *Behind* **North/South Lat.** type **N047 31
10.6620** and behind **East/West Lon.** type **E012 27
12.8377**. Remember to put the spaces at the correct positions. Behind **Altitude** type **2201** and
behind **Heading** type **310**. Then click on **OK** or
press **Enter**.

Tuning in to the right frequency

We are now at the start of runway 31 at St. Johann's
airport in Austria. We shall now tune in to the frequency of the first ADF beacon which we are going
to use. This can be done in various ways. If you
have a mouse, you can change the frequencies by
clicking on the numbers on the ADF radio. They
switch to the next number with each click.

Tuning in to the frequency

The second method is by means of the menu we used to activate the ADF. That was done by means of the **Nav/Com** menu. Select **ADF** from that menu and type the required frequency behind **ADF Frequency** in the subsequent dialog box. This is done by activating that block by clicking on it or by pressing **F**. Then simply type the frequency.

The third method is via the keyboard. Press the **A** key once. You can then change the first number of the ADF radio frequency by pressing the + and - keys. When you press the **A** key twice in succession, you can alter the second number of the frequency. Yes, you're getting the hang of it. To alter the third number, press **A** three times. In this way, we shall tune the ADF radio frequency to the **Rattenberg** beacon, which lies roughly halfway between St. Johann and Innsbruck. The frequency is **303**.

You now see that the ADF needle points approximately 60 degrees to the left. Therefore, after taking off, we must fly on a course which is 60 degrees to the left of our current course if we want to arrive at the Rattenberg beacon. Thus, the required course will be 310 (our current course) - 60 = **250 degrees**.

We're on our way!

Are you ready to begin? Position the flaps at 10
degrees because the runway is not very long, and
check that you have enough fuel. If there is no other
air traffic, we can go. After taking off, raise the landing gear and move the flaps to the original setting.
Turn leftwards. You will see that the ADF needle
moves to conform to the line of the aircraft. When it
points straight forwards, you will be travelling directly towards the beacon. We are now flying towards
the mountains. These mountains are rather high, so
climb to an altitude of 6500 feet. Make small corrections when necessary to keep the needle pointing straight forwards.

Passing the beacon

When you get nearer the beacon, the needle will become more unstable. Keep on the same course. When you fly over the beacon, you will see that the needle points backwards.

ℹ️ WHAT IS HAPPENING TO THE MANIFOLD PRESSURE?

In fact, this isn't a tip, but have you noticed that the manifold pressure is no higher than **22** although the throttle is fully open? This is because we are flying at this altitude. The lower air pressure at this height produces a lower manifold pressure than that closer to the ground.

On to the next beacon

The next beacon on our journey is quite near Innsbruck airport. It lies in fact in the same line as the runway. The frequency of this beacon is **313**, so we only need to change the middle number of the ADF radio frequency. You will see that the needle again points to the left. We have to correct our course by turning to the left in order to fly towards the beacon. Our new course is roughly **240** degrees. We follow the valley through the mountains; a river and a motorway are visible.

We have almost reached the second beacon. The runway is in sight (see the arrow)

When you have passed the beacon, steer a few degrees to the right, on a course of **265** degrees. You will pass over the town (the light area) and the runway becomes clearly visible. In your thoughts you may hear the Air Traffic Control tower informing you that you can fly a left-hand traffic pattern to land on runway 08. You can now fly a little more to the right so that the runway will appear on your left. Descend to an altitude of 1000 feet AGL. Innsbruck lies at an altitude of 1900 feet, so you can descend to an altitude of 2900 feet. Fly the traffic pattern in the same way as previously. On the final leg, the Air Traffic Control informs you (in your imagination) that you can land. You do this perfectly (we hope).

After the landing in Innsbruck (we have zoomed out to 0.50 for this picture)

Well, we made it. Our first flight using navigation beacons has taken place. You see that it's quite simple really.

In the next chapter, we shall outline how to fly using VOR beacons.

6 Navigating using the VOR

We learned how to navigate using the ADF in the previous chapter. The ADF is easy to use but it does have a few disadvantages. One of these is that the frequencies used are rather sensitive to disturbance. If, for example, there are thunderstorms in the air, the needle may point to the thunderstorm, not to the beacon. And in such situations, when you are caught in the middle of bad weather, it is very important to know exactly where you are. Another disadvantage is that it is more difficult to make corrections to compensate for the wind. If there is a crosswind, you will not fly in a straight line to the beacon; you will fly in a bend, as the figure below indicates.

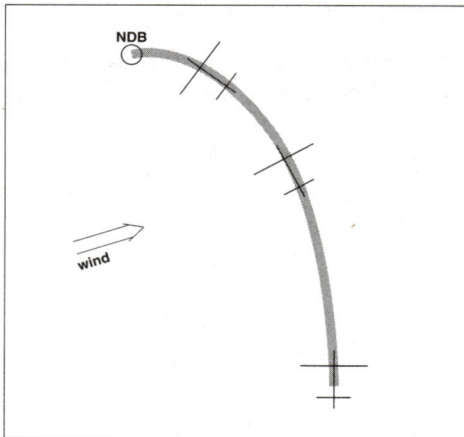

Crosswind and the ADF

The VORs are much less sensitive to disturbance
and also work more precisely. However, the principle is a little more complicated. The maps at the
back of the *Pilot's Handbook* of the Flight Simulator
show the VOR beacons (see also the pictures
below).

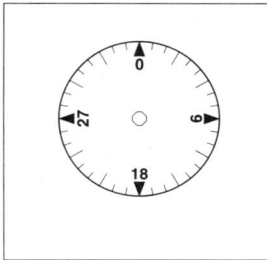

A VOR beacon

The name and the frequency are displayed in or
next to the compass dial. The VOR beacon sends
out waves in all directions. You can, as it were,
select one of these waves and follow it to or from
the beacon. Two radios are shown on the instrument panel under the communication radio COM 1
at the right-hand side. These are the VOR receivers.

NAV 1 and NAV 2

Tuning in to the NAV radio frequency

The upper one of these receivers is **NAV 1**, or
Navigation radio 1; the second of these is, not sur-
prisingly, **NAV 2**. Changing the frequencies of these
is done in exactly the same way as with the ADF.
The first method of doing this is via the **Nav/Com**
menu. Then select **Navigation Radios**. You can type
the new frequency as you did with the ADF: click
on the block or press **F**. Then enter the frequency.
Subsequently click on **OK** or press **Enter**. The new
frequency is shown on the NAV 1 radio. In order to
change the frequency of the second NAV radio,
press **R** (or click on the corresponding block) in the
Navigation Radios dialog window.

The second method of changing the frequency is by
pressing **N** and then **1** or **2** for respectively the NAV
1 or NAV 2 radio. Then you can change the num-
bers before the decimal point by pressing the **+** and
- keys. To change numbers behind the decimal
point, press **N** twice in succession. The numbers
behind the point become yellow and you can
change them by pressing the **+** and **-** keys.

The final and easiest way of tuning in is by means of
the mouse. Click on the required radio and then
simply press the left mouse button. This changes the
frequency. If you keep the mouse pointer to the left
of the number shown, a lower frequency is selected
with each click; if you place the pointer to the right
of the number, a higher frequency is selected. This
applies to numbers both in front of and behind the
decimal point.

The easiest way of explaining all this is using a practical example.

Paris

We shall use the VOR beacons to make a flight from Orly Airport near Paris to Beauvais which lies about 100 miles to the north of Paris. We shall move to runway 08 at Orly. This takes place in the familiar way via the **World** menu and the **Set Exact location** option. Behind **North/South Lat.** type **N048 43 14.7066** and behind **East/West Lon.** type **E002 21 37.6238**. The **Altitude** should be **295**, the height of the airport above sea level. Type **80** behind **Heading**; this is the magnetic direction of runway 08. Then click on **OK** or press **Enter**.

A map of the relevant part of France is shown on page 225 of the Flight Simulator *Pilot's Handbook*. Page 227 displays a map of Orly airport. A simplified map of the places and beacons we shall discuss is shown overleaf.

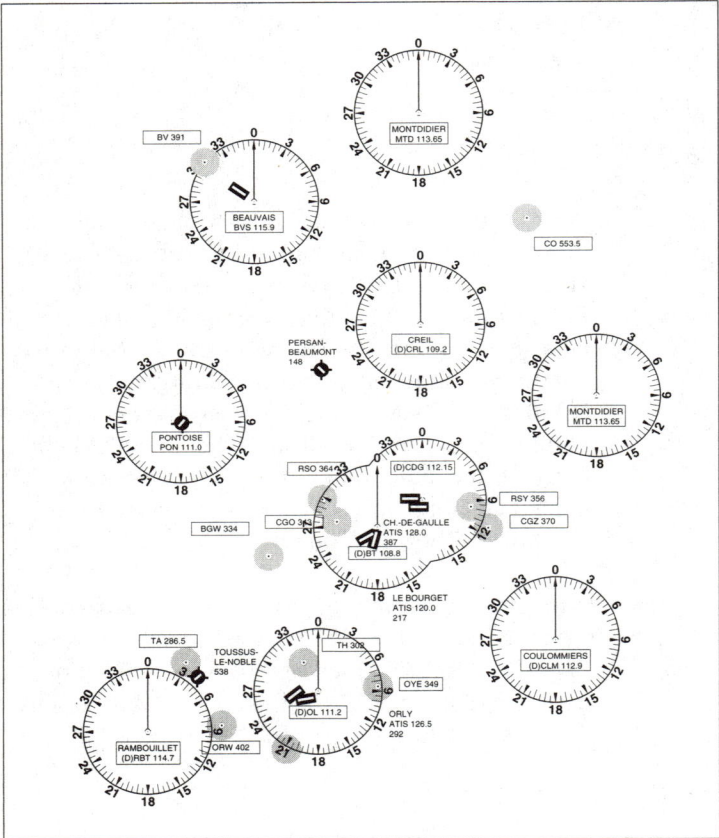

We are now situated at the beginning of runway 08 at Orly airport. Before proceeding further, we shall remove from the screen the ADF dial which replaced the bottom VOR instrument. (You may have already changed your screen.) Open the **Nav/Com** menu and select **ADF**. Press **A** to deactivate the ADF radio.

Tuning in the VORs

The first beacon which we shall make use of is to the north of Paris, at Creil (CRL). The frequency of this VOR is 109.2 MHz. Tune in your NAV 1 radio in one of the ways we have just discussed. The next beacon we shall use is BVS which lies to the north-west of CRL. Can you find the appropriate frequency? Yes, it's 115.9 MHz. You can specify this frequency on your NAV 2 radio.

We now have to specify the **radial** we want to fly from Orly to CRL. A radial is a magnetic course you follow in relation to the ground. The two VOR instruments are to the right of the other flying instruments. The **V1** button at the left of the upper dial enables you to select the radial you need.

Look at the figure showing the VORs, either on the previous page or in the *Pilot's Handbook*. The small blocks or rectangles represent the airport runways. Now take a ruler and draw a line from Orly to the CRL beacon. You will see that, in the compass dial around Orly, the line you draw passes through the longer stripe to the right of the arrow indicating north. Each of the longer stripes in this dial represents 10 degrees, the shorter stripes represent 5 degrees. This means that you will have to fly on a radial of 10 degrees to get from Orly to the CRL beacon.

The easiest way of selecting a radial is again using the mouse. Click on the **V1** button. You see that each click raises (click to the right of the number) or lowers (left) the numbers shown.

The second way of selecting a radial is via the
Nav/Com menu. Then choose **Navigation Radios**.
You can select the required radial behind **OBS
Heading**. You activate this line by pressing **O** (at
NAV 1); for NAV 2, this is the letter **H**. The box
becomes black and you can then type the radial.
Confirm the radial setting by clicking on **OK** or by
pressing **OK**.

The third and last method is via the keyboard. Press
the **V** and then **1** (for NAV 1) or the **2** (NAV 2). You
can then change the radial shown by means of the
+ and **-** keys.

Thus, select the radial 10 degrees on **NAV 1** and
radial **312** on **NAV 2**.

NAV 1 and NAV 2, with the selected frequencies

You will now see that the word **TO** is shown in the
dial of the upper VOR. This means that when you
follow a course of 10 degrees, you will fly straight
towards the beacon if the white needle is in the
middle. If the needle moves to the left for example,
due to the wind or because you don't hold course,
you will have to steer to the left to get back on the

required radial. You will see that the needle is currently to the right of the middle, but once we have taken off, it will automatically move to the middle.

Into the air

Let's get going. We have permission from the Air Traffic Control to take off. We are also advised to climb to a height of 1500 feet and we should turn off towards Creil when we reach an altitude of 3000 feet.

Therefore, when we take off, we have to keep to the current course of 080 degrees. While doing this, have a look at the needle in the first VOR. It keeps on moving to the left bit by bit. This means that we are steadily approaching the selected radial. The figure below gives an indication of how this takes place.

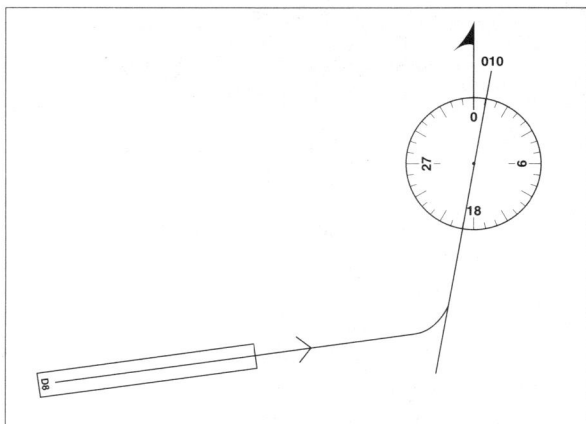

Steadily approaching the selected radial

When we reach 1500 feet, the needle is exactly in the middle. We can now switch course left, to 10 degrees. In the turn you will probably hear a broken beep tone and a yellow **M** light will appear. Pay no attention to this, there's nothing wrong. This is a part of an approach procedure for a different runway.

Paris. The Eiffel Tower seems to have shrunk

When you are on the radial you will see a river in front of you. That is the famous Seine. If you now look out of the left window, you will have a delightful view of the centre of Paris. Can you see the Eiffel tower? Make sure that the VOR needle remains in the middle. If it moves a little to the left, compensate by also turning to the left until you are on the radial again. If the needle moves to the right, turn the plane a bit to the right.

When we fly a distance further, we come to a rather busy area. This is an area between two airports. The Le Bourget airport lies to our left and a little further on to our right lies the Charles de Gaulle airport. Keep looking around you to make sure you don't get too near other aircraft.

Perhaps you can see the Charles de Gaulle airport through the window at the right-hand side. When we pass this airport, the scenery becomes greener. The greyness of the city is left behind and we come ever closer to our beacon. Just before we reach the beacon you will be able to see another airport in the distance. This is Persan-Beaumont. You will also notice that, just as with the ADF, the needle becomes more unstable as we approach the beacon. This is because the radials are now nearer one another as it were. At the moment we pass the beacon, the word **TO** in the NAV 1 radio changes to **FR** (for From). If we now keep on following a course of 10 degrees, the current radial, we shall not arrive at the desired destination. Therefore we should now switch over to the radial to fly us to the next beacon, BVS.

We have already selected the proper frequency on the second radio, but you can also select it on the first radio if you prefer. Do not forget to specify the appropriate radial, 312 to BVS. Then you will see that we are on our way **TO** the BVS beacon on a course of 312 degrees (plus or minus wind correction). Make a left turn to latch on to the new course and make small corrections to keep the needle in the middle of the dial.

The airport comes into sight after about 4 minutes.
This map indicates that the beacon is in front of the
airport, at a distance of roughly two miles. We can
now slowly descend to the traffic pattern altitude.
The airport lies at an altitude of 358 feet above sea
level. We add 1000 feet to this, which means we
can descend to an altitude of 1400 feet for the traffic pattern. This time we have to fly a right-hand circuit instead of a left-hand one. We are to touch
down on runway 13. This means that we have to
shift course a little to the left so that the runway is
on our right. We shall then land in the opposite
direction to that in which we are now flying. This
should be no problem to you at this stage. Do your
best.

Points to note when using the VOR

You may think that it seems complicated using the
VOR, but the opposite is the case. It's only a question of getting used to it. We have jotted down a
few points you should keep in mind:

■   If you select a radial by means of the OBS (but-
    ton V1 or V2), you in fact divide the VOR com-
    pass dial into 4 sections. As an example, we shall
    use the 000 or 360 radial (see the figure below).

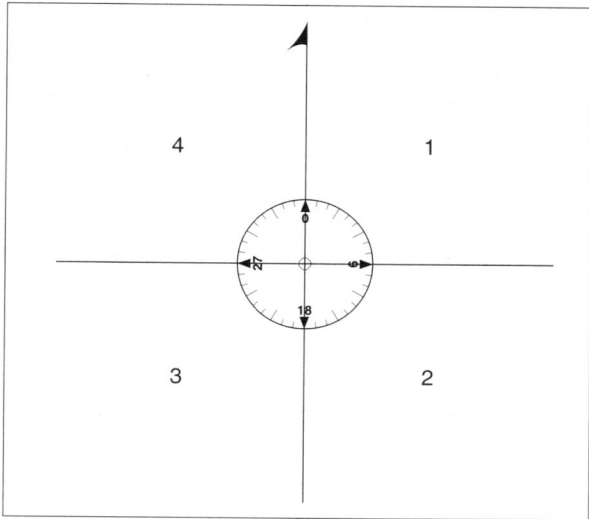

The compass dial with radial 000

If you are flying in the area containing the 1, the needle points to the left and the TO/FR indicator will display **FR**. This is because, if you are flying to the north (360 degrees course), you will have to fly to the left to get on to the selected radial. Once you are on the radial and you continue flying a course of 360 degrees, you will be flying away from the beacon. Keep in mind that the actual course of the aircraft has nothing to do with the figures shown on the VOR. The VOR does not know in which direction you wish to go. It only gives an indication of the **quadrant** in which you are flying, in other words, your relationship to the beacon. If you are flying in the second quadrant, the VOR indications are as follows: the needle is pointing to the left because you have to correct your course by flying

to the left, and TO is displayed because you are flying in the direction of the beacon if your course is
360 degrees (not counting any correction for the
wind). You will be able to work out for yourself
what the indications will be when you are flying in
segments 3 and 4. In segment 3 the needle will
point to the right and the VOR will display TO. In
segment 4, the needle will also point to the right but
FR will be displayed.

In fact, we have not applied the terms absolutely
correctly in this explanation. The word **radial** actually refers to the waves being emitted from the radio
station. But if you come from the north and are flying towards the beacon, you will select **180** degrees
on the OBS because that is the course **towards** the
beacon. However, you will latch on to the 360
degree radial to get there. Therefore keep in mind:
the radials are transmitted **from** the beacon. If you
are flying **to** the beacon, your course is 180 degrees
opposite.

As we mentioned, the theory is quite complicated.
But you will have noticed that, in practice, it's not
difficult at all.
Now that we know how the VOR and the ADF
work, we can use them in situations, for example, in
which we have lost our way.

7 Help, we are lost!

When flying from one airfield to another, we try, of course, to keep a good idea of our position. Nevertheless, it is quite easy to lose track of our exact location, due perhaps to the fact that we are flying over a large area with few landmarks. But even when you are flying over familiar ground, it is easy to lose your way if the visibility is poor.

I personally once flew with a trainee pilot in a night with poor visibility. We took off from a small airport in North Carolina in the USA. We practised various routines for roughly three quarters of an hour and then I asked him to fly us back to the airport. The runway was situated alongside a motorway. After looking around for a bit, the trainee spotted the motorway. He thought he knew where we were and followed the motorway for a while. You can guess what happened - it turned out to be the wrong motorway. There happened to be another small runway alongside this motorway too. Just when the trainee began to doubt whether all was well, he saw the light beacon of the airport. He flew a neat circuit and he only noticed something strange when we touched down! A completely unknown airport! Thus, as you see, a mistake is easily made, even by trained flyers. This was a good lesson.

We shall use an example to illustrate how to find your way back to a particular spot.

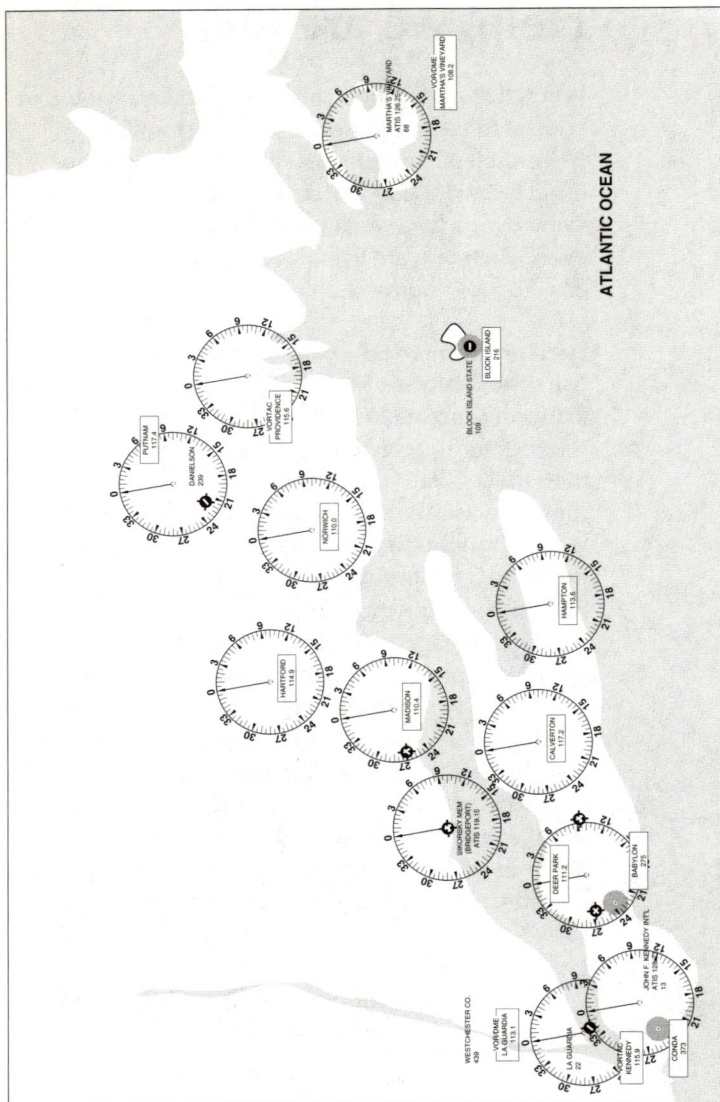

Back to America

Imagine we have planned a flight from Westchester County in New York State to Martha's Vineyard. You will see on the map that almost the entire route is over water which offers few points of recognition. Nevertheless, we wish to fly over the water since that is the shortest route and, after all, we are not too far out from the coast if anything should go wrong. We have measured that the distance from one airport to the other is 135 miles. The average speed will be 120 knots, so that the flight should take something like an hour and eight minutes.

We take off and everything seems to be going fine. But unfortunately the visibility is worse than we expected and we are no longer sure that we are on the right course. We haven't seen the coast for some time, although that is no reason for discomfort. But we should be flying over water. We have been flying for about 50 minutes and therefore Long Island is behind us, but we should have seen Block Island to the right by now. However, there is no trace of it as yet. Are we lost?

In the clouds

To make the situation we have just described a bit more realistic, we shall give the position to which the aircraft should go (not the exact latitude and longitude) and we shall create some cloudy weather. In this way, you don't have to fly the whole trip up to the point that we get lost.

We shall first create the clouds. That is done as follows. Open the **World** menu and select **Weather**. We are already familiar with this dialog window. Normally the **Clouds** option button will be activated. This enables you to create all sorts of clouds, even thunder. The button under Clouds is **Winds**. We are also familiar with this option from the time we practised landing with crosswind. You will also see that the temperature and the air pressure (Baro) can be altered.

We shall proceed with **Clouds**, which is already activated. Click on the **Create** button (or press **R**). We can now begin creating our own clouds. This is done as follows. Behind **Base**, type **6000**. This means that the bottom of the clouds is at an altitude of 6000 feet. Now type **10000** behind **Tops**. Thus, the cloud layer is 4000 feet thick. Open the **Coverage** option by clicking on it or by pressing **C**. Click on the arrow pointing downwards until you see Overcast (or press the Cursor Down key). Click on Overcast or mark it and press Enter. This means that the sky is fully overcast. If you were to choose **Scatter 4/8**, the sky would be half-covered with cloud.

```
                    Create Cloud Layer
                                          ┌──────────┐
                                          │    OK    │
Type:           Clouds  ▾                 │  Cancel  │
Base (ft MSL): 005999                     └──────────┘
Tops (ft MSL): 010001
Coverage:       Overcast ▾
Deviation (ft): 000000
```

The Create Cloud Layer dialog box

Now click on **OK** or press **Enter**. You return to the **Weather** menu. Click on the specifications you

have just made (**005999 to 10001 Overcast**) in the
Cloud Layers box. Click on **OK** or press **Enter**. The
clouds appear in the sky just as you programmed
them. You can gain the most realistic effect as follows. Open the **Options** menu and select
Preferences. Then choose the **Display** button from
the subsequent dialog window. See if there is a
cross next to **Textured Sky**. If that is not the case,
press **X** or click on the appropriate box with the
mouse. The clouds will now look much more realistic, but it does require more computer memory to
display them in this way. Click on **OK**.

We now get lost

Open the **World** menu and select **Set Exact
Location**. Now click on the small circle in front of
Set Location with X/Z coordinates or press **X**.
Behind **North**, type **17395.9650** and behind **East**,
type **21921.7565**. You already know how this
works. Behind **Region** you should see **USA**. Specify
3000 behind **Altitude**. Type **097** behind **Heading**
since this is the direction you calculated from
Westchester Point to Martha's Vineyard. Then click
on **OK** or press **Enter**, and you move instantly to the
specified ('lost') location. Keep in mind that you are
flying immediately, so place the rudder and ailerons
in position, open the throttle and make sure the
landing gear has been raised.

This looks pretty lost

It all looks quite blue and grey around us. It makes little difference which way we look. We should have passed Block Island a few minutes ago, but we haven't seen it yet. Maybe we should have followed the coastline after all. However, we're not going to give up or bale out yet. We cannot just keep on flying above the sea, that is the way to the pearly gates.

Look at the map to see where the beacons are located. There is a beacon called **Norwich** to the northwest of Block Island. We shall tune our first VOR into its frequency. The map indicates that the required frequency is **110.00 MHz**. Remember how to select it? Either click on the number in NAV 1 or open the **Nav/Com** menu and select **Navigation**

Radios; type the required Frequency. We shall now examine which radial of that beacon we are on. In a real aeroplane it's not possible to simply take a break, but it is possible in the Flight Simulator. Press **P**.

Cross reference

Turn the OBS selector until you have centred the needle on the first VOR and **FR** is displayed in the dial. This can best be done by clicking on the **V1** button at the bottom left of the dial; the numbers change and the needle moves. You can also press **V** and centre the needle by pressing the **+** or **-** keys. You will see that the needle becomes centred somewhere in the neighbourhood of radial **153**. (This will depend on how long you fly onwards before making these specifications.)

You now have to find out your exact position on the radial. There are two ways of doing this. You can tune your second VOR to a different beacon and see which radial of that beacon you are on. If you draw lines from the beacons along these two radials (on VOR1 and VOR2), the place where they cross will represent your current position.

We shall set the second VOR to the most easterly beacon on Long Island. Can you find it on the map? It is called **Hampton** and its frequency is **113.60 MHz**. Proceed in the same way as with the first VOR (click on V2 or press V and then 2). Adjust the OBS selector of the second VOR until the needle is centred and **FR** is displayed in the dial. If you have done this correctly, the needle will be centred on a radial of roughly **096** from Hampton VOR.

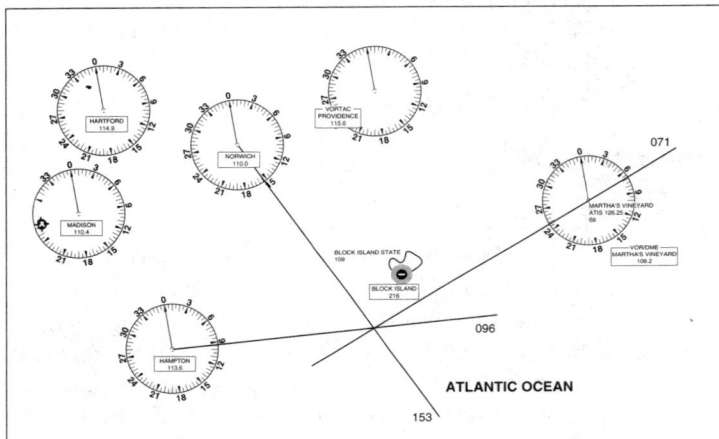

Now draw the two radials on the map at the back of the *Pilot's Handbook*. As mentioned, your position is where these lines cross one another. Now you will be able to see that you have passed Block Island, but it is to your left instead of to the right.

You could have discovered this in another, perhaps easier way. The VOR stations we use here also give a **distance indication**. You will see a measuring instrument to the right of the NAV 1 radio. This shows DME which is an abbreviation for Distance Measuring Equipment. Thus, this is the distance from the plane to the VOR station. In this case, you are 43.5 miles from the Norwich VOR, on a radial of 153. This is a very easy and convenient way of determining your position.

And now on to Martha's Vineyard

At your present altitude there is probably a reasonably strong northerly wind. This will push you southwards. Press the **Scroll Lock** key and then **1** on the
numeric keypad. You now look diagonally backwards and you can see Block Island. Whew! At least
we know where we are.

But how do we get to our destination, Martha's
Vineyard? Any idea? If you look at the map, you will
see that there is also a VOR at Martha's Vineyard.
Of course, this is ideal for finding the shortest way
to the airfield. By the way, the frequency of this
VOR is not 108.2 MHz as given in the *Pilot's
Handbook,* it is **114.5 MHz**. Tune your NAV 1 radio
to this frequency. Then turn the OBS selector until
the needle is centred and you have a TO indication
on the dial. You will see that you have to fly a
course of 071 to fly towards the beacon. Therefore,
we turn to the left. The DME shows that we are
41.3 miles from the VOR.

Press **P** to release the Paused situation. We shall
again set course to our destination. We continue
with a manifold pressure of 18 and a speed of
approximately 120 knots. Press the **F** key and then
+ or **-**. If you now click on the DME instrument, it no
longer shows the distance to the beacon, it shows
your speed in relation to the ground. To do the
same for the second VOR, press **F** and then **2**. The
rest is exactly the same. In the meantime, you will
see the island appear in front of you.

The communication radio

Now we wish to know which runway at the airport
is in use. We can find out by tuning the communication radio to the relevant frequency. The COM
radio is in the instrument panel above the VOR
receivers. The communication frequency for the airport is **126.25 MHz**. You can select this in various
ways too. The easiest way is to use the mouse. If
you click on the figures in front of the decimal
point, they will increase or decrease by one with
each click. If you click to the left of the number, it
decreases; if you click to the right, it increases by
one. The same principle applies to the decimals. A
second way of doing this is by means of the
Nav/Com menu. Select the **Communication Radio**
option. Press **F** and type the required frequency
behind COM 1 Frequency. Then click on **OK** or
press **Enter**. The third and final method is by means
of the keyboard. Press **C** once. You will see that the
part of the frequency in front of the decimal point is
displayed in yellow. You can now use the **+** and **-**
keys to change the numbers. Press **C** twice in succession to change the numbers behind the point.
Information suddenly appears on the bar under the
cockpit window. This deals with the weather and
the runway in use.

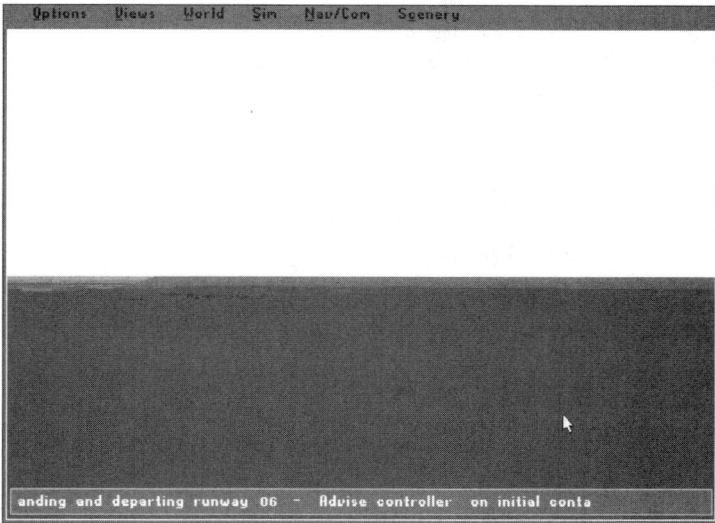

The Automatic Terminal Information Service

This is the **ATIS**, which stands for **Automatic Terminal Information Service**. What was that information exactly? *Martha's Vineyard - Information X-ray 14:00 zulu weather - Measured ceiling 6000 overcast, Visibility 10 - Temperature 74 F - Winds calm - Altimeter 30.15 - Landing and departing runway 06 - Advise controller on initial contact you have X-ray.*

You were probably not able to follow this all the first time around. If you want to read it again, press **C** and everything is shown again. But what does it all mean? The information given is generally record-ed on a tape which is continually played at a certain frequency. Each time that the weather changes suffi-ciently to require a new tape, a new version is recorded with a new letter code. In practice, this means that the tape is altered at least every half hour. For this tape, the letter code is an **X**. At the back of this book, there is a paragraph containing the ICAO alphabet in the Appendix. In aviation, letters are expressed by using words or terms so that the chance of mistakes or confusion is reduced as much as possible. (With poor reception the letter N sounds like M for example.) This paragraph indicates that the letter X is expressed by the term **X ray**. Then the time is stated when the message was recorded. In this case, that was 14.00 hours. The time used in aviation is **GMT**, Greenwich Mean Time. This is often referred to as **zulu time**. Nowadays this is officially called **UTC**, Universal Coordinated Time. Then comes the weather report. The cloud base begins at 6000 feet - we know this, after all, we programmed it ourselves. Then the visibility and the temperature are given. This is still given in Fahrenheit in America. 74F is roughly 23 Centigrade (Celsius). Then the wind is given; this doesn't amount to much. The **Altimeter setting** is quite important. We already mentioned that the altimeter is in fact a barometer. If the air pressure on the ground changes, you have to compensate for that otherwise the altimeter will display the wrong information.

We shall examine the consequences of this. Open the **Sim** menu and select **Calibrate Altimeter**.

Calibrate Altimeter		
Current Pressure (in Hg): 30.15		OK
(millibars): 1021		Cancel
Barometric Pressure (in Hg):	30.15	
Barometric Pressure (millibars):	1021	

The Calibrate Altimeter dialog box

Then press **B** and you can now type the current altimeter setting. Thus, in this situation, type 30.15 as shown in the weather report. In Europe, especially on the continent, the altimeter setting is always given in **millibars** or **hectoPascal**. You can enter any specification of this type on the bottom line by pressing the **A**. Then click on **OK**. The altimeter will now indicate the correct height.

The next line (Landing and departing runway 06) is self-explanatory, and the last line means that you should communicate to the controller that you have received the 'X ray' information. Then the controller knows that you are aware of the weather situation and which runway is in use. Good, we are gradually approaching the airport and we know that we shall land on runway 06. This happens to be roughly in the same direction as we are now flying. This time we shall approach the final leg directly instead of following the whole traffic pattern. We refer to this as the **Straight in approach**.

When the DME instrument shows 10 miles, we shall alter our course a little to the right so that we approach the runway directly. Hold a course of 090 degrees. You can begin descending simultaneously, otherwise you will be too high for the runway shortly. You will now see the airfield appear in front of you to the left. Hold a course of 090 degrees until you are on the line of the runway, and then turn left on to a course of 060 degrees. (The exact line of the runway is 056 degrees.) When you get closer to the runway, you will be able to see the lights at the left-hand side of the runway which indicate whether you are flying to high or too low. These are the

VASI lights which we discussed previously. When
the DME instrument shows 5 miles, you should be
at an altitude of roughly 1500 feet. At a distance of
3 miles, you should be at 900 feet. You can follow
the VASI lights from that moment onwards. Do not
forget to lower the landing gear, check that the flaps
are in the proper position and get ready to land.
When you have landed, you will see a taxiway at
right angles to the runway on which you landed.
Turn right here, go to the end and turn right again.
You will see Air Traffic Control. Go a little further
and park in the box with the F (activate the map by
pressing Num Lock).

Well, that was quite exciting and we did find the airport after all. In the next chapters, we shall learn
how to fly when the weather is even worse. In that
case, you will be able to find your way to the airport
using the instruments only.

8 Flying blind

When we learned to fly, we learned that you can fly almost without having to look at your instruments. After opening the throttle fully and ensuring that the nose is in the proper position, you know that the aeroplane will climb at a certain speed. In reverse, it is also possible to fly using the instruments only, without having to look out the window. Even in the relatively small Cessna, there are enough devices to get you from one airport to another even if the cloud base is very low and you have to fly with almost no visibility. Officially, this is referred to as flying under **IFR**, which stands for **Instrument Flight Rules**. You have to keep to the rules when you are flying blindly through the clouds. This is referred to as **IMC**, which stands for **Instrument Meteorological Conditions**. In this chapter, we shall learn to fly all over again, but this time only using the instruments. We shall make a complete flight in the next chapter.

Flying blind in California

We shall move to **California**, to the **Van Nuys** airport, for the following exercise. You now know how to do that, but we shall provide the relevant information anyway. Open the **World** menu and select **Airports**. You will see the **Choose a scenery area** option at the top. Click on this option or press **C**. Select **USA - Los Angeles**. You are presented with a list of airports in that area. The bottom line is **Van Nuys - Runway 16R**. Select this (click or use the Cursor Down key and Enter) and you are whisked

off to the airfield straightaway. The **R** in the name
means that there are two runways and you are on
the right-hand one.

We shall now create some cloud layers. We learned
how this was done in the previous chapter. Open
the **World** menu and select **Weather**. Choose
Clouds and **Create**. We can now create the cloud
layer. Behind **Base**, type **2000**, and behind **Tops**,
type **4000**. Behind **Coverage**, select **Overcast**. Now
click on **OK** or press **Enter**. The first cloud layer has
now been programmed.
To make the second layer, select **Create** once
more. Behind **Base**, type 6000, and behind **Tops**,
type **10000**. Select **Overcast** again.

We have now created two cloud layers, one from
2000 to 4000 feet and the other from 6000 to
10000 feet. There are no clouds between 4000 and
6000 feet, and above 10000 feet there is blue sky.
Before clicking on **OK** in the Weather dialog box,
check if there are other cloud layers. If so, mark
them by clicking on them or moving the cursor bar
to them, and then activate the Delete button. The
computer will ask you if you really want to delete
the selected cloud layer. Click on **OK** or press
Enter.

A few preparations first

Before taking off, we shall make a few preparations
so that we don't have to be so busy once we are
airborne. You can begin by selecting the frequency
113.1 MHz on VOR 1. This is the frequency of the

VOR at the airport so that we can find our way back. And you can also select radial **341** on the OBS or VOR 1, since we shall need this shortly.

We said that we would learn to fly all over again. You will have to read all the information on your instruments once you are in the clouds; looking out the window won't help at all. The intestines of a cloud are not very interesting. But there are many instruments supplying lots of information and it is quite difficult to learn to look at the right instrument at exactly the right time.

The flying instruments are right in front of you. These, along with the engine instruments, indicate what an aeroplane is doing at any given time. We can explain this all in rather complex theoretical terms, but the best way to learn is by doing it. This is the great advantage of the Flight Simulator: you can try things out which are just not possible in a real plane. If, for instance, anything goes wrong, you can simply press the **P** and you can work out your problem calmly and methodically.

Shall we give it a go? We get permission from Air Traffic Control to take off. We shall climb to an altitude of 5000 feet, keeping to the same compass direction as the runway, which means a course of 161 degrees. Place the flaps in the take-off position (10 degrees, press F6) and check the engine instruments. If everything is in order, we can go.

The first part takes place as we are used to; we can still look around us, but try to concentrate more on the instruments once you have raised the landing gear and have brought the flaps into the normal flying position.

To what should we pay attention?

While climbing

First check the **artificial horizon**. It shows whether or not the wings are horizontal in relation to the horizon. If the wings are horizontal, this means that you are not making a turn. You can also check this by examining the **heading indicator** to see if your course is still 161 degrees. Thus, the most important instrument for checking that you are flying in a straight line is the artificial horizon; it indicates whether or not you are banking. To confirm this, check the **heading indicator** to see if you are still on course.

The other instrument which is very important in this stage of the flight is the **airspeed indicator**. This will inform you whether the pitch is correct or not. If the speed is too low, the nose position is too high, and if the speed is too high, the nose position is too low. Try to climb, as we did previously, at a speed of 80 knots and hold a course of 161 degrees. If you have to make corrections, it is important to make small adjustments, otherwise you will overcompensate and you will quickly go from bad to worse.

In the meantime, we have reached the clouds. It is quite strange at first not to be able to see the ground or the horizon. But you will quickly get used to it. Make sure that the wings remain parallel to the horizon; information about the **pitch** (the nose position) can be gained by looking at the airspeed indicator: speed too high, nose too low and vice versa. Make small corrections where necessary and wait

until the instruments have stabilised before making
further corrections.

We leave the first layer of cloud at an altitude of
4000 feet, but you will see the second layer above
you. We shall level off at an altitude of 5000 feet
just as we have always done. If we keep on climbing at 80 knots, we shall climb at a rate of 800 feet
per minute. This means that 80 feet before we get
to an altitude of 5000 feet, we should adjust the
pitch to level off. This will mean that the speed
increases. When you reach 120 knots, close the
throttle a little so that the manifold pressure
becomes roughly 18. The speed then remains constant at 120 knots. We wish to keep on flying
straight ahead at an altitude of 5000 feet.

While flying straight ahead

You can probably guess what has now become the
most important instrument. Yes, the artificial horizon. Just as during the climb, you can check whether or not you are banking and turning. You can confirm this by looking at your heading indicator. The
most important instrument for determining the pitch
is the **altimeter**, in conjunction with the vertical
speed indicator. If you are still climbing, the pitch is
too high; if you are descending, the pitch is too low.
Try just to fly at an altitude of 5000 feet on a course
of 161 degrees. Keep an eye on the appropriate
instruments. We refer to this as **scanning**. Make
small corrections where necessary. If it all gets too
confusing or out of control, simply press **P** and take
the time to think out what you have to do. That is
what the simulator is all about.

While making a turn

If you are now able to fly straight forwards, it's time
to practise making turns. Normally, when flying
blind, you would only make gentle turns. You will
see two stripes at the right- and left-hand sides of
the turn coordinator in the lower left-hand corner of
the instrument panel. The upper two indicate that
you are flying straight forwards. The lower stripes
indicate that you are making a **standard rate turn**.
This means that you are banking in such a way that
it will take two minutes to make a complete turn.
The faster you fly, the more steep the bank will have
to be to complete the turn in two minutes. And how
can you know how much you have to bank to perform a standard rate turn? Well, there's a simple
trick for remembering this. Take your **True Airspeed**
(in the Flight Simulator that is the speed on the
speedometer; in a real plane this need not always
be the case), divide it by 10 and then add 5. This
produces the angle you have to bank to make a
standard rate turn.

You can make small adjustments by referring to the
turn coordinator. In our particular case, the angle of
inclination should be 120/10 + 5 = **17** degrees.
Thus, if we want to make a standard rate turn when
flying at a speed of 120 knots, we have to bank at
an angle of 17 degrees. Let's try this out.

We shall first make a complete standard rate turn to
the left. We begin by rolling to the left. The artificial
horizon indicates the angle of bank. In this case, the
pointer almost comes to the second stripe, which
represents an angle of 20 degrees. We then look at

the turn coordinator to see if we really are flying a standard rate turn. If this is not the case, make small adjustments. Keep an eye on the altimeter to ensure that we do not gain or lose too much altitude.

Is there any future?

Check your heading indicator now and again to see if you're getting round to the original direction again. Use the same formula to roll out of the turn as we used previously. Begin rolling out when you reach the half of the angle of inclination before the required direction. In this case, that is the half of 17 degrees, Therefore, we should begin rolling out 9 degrees before we reach a course of 161 degrees. In our case, that is when we reach 170 degrees. We shall do the same exercise again, but this time we shall make a right-hand turn. If that is also suc-

cessful, try making a left-hand turn followed immediately by a right-hand turn.

We keep on keeping on

If this exercise was also successful, you are ready for
the next one. Get back on to a course of 161 if you
have deviated. We shall now climb to an altitude of
8000 feet at a constant speed. We open the throttle
fully and raise the pitch of the aircraft. We shall
climb at a rate of 500 feet per minute. The **vertical
speed indicator** now provides the most important
information concerning the pitch of the plane. If
you are climbing too quickly, lower the pitch a little
and if the climb takes too long, raise the pitch. You
will probably have to make small adjustments continually, otherwise you will move through the air
like a dolphin through water. Keep a close watch on
the vertical speed indicator. It reacts rather slowly
and it takes some time before it becomes stable. If
you are also keeping an eye on the speedometer,
you will see that the speed has decreased. This is
because the air becomes thinner at greater altitudes
and for this reason the engine has less power. In
order to keep on climbing at the same speed, raise
the pitch bit by bit, although the speed does
decrease.

Back to the airfield

When you are at 8000 feet, you can close the throttle a little to create a manifold pressure of 18. Your
eyes will have become tired due to all the concen-

tration on the instruments. It takes a lot of effort at first to obtain a good scan, but after a while you will get used to looking at the proper instruments at the proper time. Make a turn to the left or the right so that you come out on a course of 340 degrees. Before we took off, we set our VOR to the 341 radial. This will bring us back to the runway. The frequency of the VOR at the runway is 113.10 MHz. Check that you are still tuned to it. Now examine where the needle is. If it is to the right of the middle, you will have to steer to the right to get on the radial. If the needle is to the left, steer to the left. Do this by altering the course 30 degrees to the right or the left. When the needle is exactly in the middle, you can fly a course of 341 degrees, making small corrections for the wind.

The DME indicates your distance from the airfield. We have been flying around for quite some time so it is probably reasonably far to the VOR. Therefore, there is no need as yet to fly lower than 8000 feet. In the meantime, the Air Traffic Control will inform you that runway 34 is being used. This is convenient because we can land in the same direction as we are now travelling. Try to make a plan for descending. We are now at 8000 feet.

Going down

When going down, you should descend at a rate of 1000 feet for every three miles. You are now flying at 8000 feet, so you should begin descending 24 miles before your destination. The descent should take place at a rate of 500 feet per minute. Air

Traffic Control indicates that you can descend to an
altitude of 2300 feet. If you descend at a constant
rate of descent, the vertical speed indicator is the
most important instrument for indicating pitch information. If you are descending at a constant speed,
the airspeed indicator is the most important instrument for indicating pitch information. In both cases,
the heading indicator is the most important instrument for indicating whether you are still flying
straight forwards or not.

When the DME shows 10 miles, reduce the throttle
to produce a manifold pressure of 16. Your speed
will decrease to roughly 100 knots. When the DME
shows 5.5 miles, place the flaps in a position of 10
degrees and lower the landing gear. At 5 miles,
begin descending at a rate of 500 feet per minute.
Keep an eye on the VOR instrument to ensure that
you are still on the 341 radial. Air Traffic Control
indicates that you can descend to an altitude of
1200 feet.

Remember that this is only 400 feet above the
ground! The cloud base is 2000 feet, so you will be
able to see the runway clearly. Can you see the
VASI lights already, to the left of the runway? As
soon as you come out of the clouds and see the
runway, you can follow the VASI lights and descend
under the 1200 feet. Air Traffic Control gives you
permission to land.

So, we have completed our first 'blind flight'. You
can again park to the left of the runway in the yellow square so that the fuel tanks can be replen-
ished. You have just proved that it is also possible to

fly in the clouds in a small aircraft, knowing exactly where you are and the precise angle of flight.

Another blind flight exercise

In order to give you more expertise in blind flying, we shall now work through an exercise which can be carried out from any airport. This exercise is aimed at improving your coordination and spreading your attention across the diverse instruments. At the same time, this exercise resembles the various approach procedures you use when the visibility is poor or the cloud base low. This exercise (and exercises like this one) is used in many flight training colleges both in the simulator and in real aircraft.

In addition to the basic exercises we have just performed, you will now combine various elements. For instance, you will climb or descend while turning. This will seem quite difficult at first, but try to divide your attention equally across the instruments and if you have to make adjustments, make small ones so that the plane does not become unstable due to overcompensation. You can also make small variations to your flight pattern so that you can practise those manoeuvres with which you have the most difficulty. Make sure you have enough altitude before beginning the exercise. The figure below shows the pattern you will fly.

A very useful exercise

We begin by flying straight forwards for one minute. Flying due north is the easiest. After one minute, change your course 45 degrees to the left. Keep to this course, 315 degrees, for one more minute and then make a turn of 180 degrees to the right. The new course is thus 135 degrees. After half a minute, turn right again, on to a course of 180 degrees. Once you are on this course, descend at a rate of 500 feet per minute until you have descended a thousand feet: therefore, two minutes descent. Then make an ascending turn to the right, on a course of 225 degrees and keep climbing until you reach the original altitude. Make a left turn to get on a course due north once again, and then make a right turn on to a course of 180 degrees. Hold this course for a minute and then turn right again to get on a northerly course once again.

This pattern closely resembles the pattern you would fly when approaching a runway when the visibility is poor. You would use the first part, straight forwards, to pass a beacon on the airfield for example. The first turn is referred to as a **procedure turn**, and then you descend to come out of the clouds; you fly the rest of the procedure when the visibility is so poor or the cloud base so low that you cannot see the runway. This section is referred to as the **missed approach procedure**. The last part is the so-called **holding procedure**. When you can master this exercise, you are ready to move on to the next chapter in which we shall make a complete flight in bad conditions with poor visibility and low cloud. We have to make the whole flight relying exclusively on our instruments. Are you ready?

9 Navigating through the clouds

You are now well on your way to becoming an expert pilot. We shall now fly from a very busy airport in Chicago, O'Hare, to Champaign in Illinois. We have become familiar with Chicago to a certain extent: each time we start up the Flight Simulator, we begin at Meig's Field which is a little smaller. Have a look at the map in the *Pilot's Handbook* (page 212). The large Chicago airport is to the northwest of the city and is one of the busiest airports in the world. Our destination, Champaign, is in the same state (Illinois) but a good deal further south.

Going to the point of departure

The first thing we have to do is to move to the relevant airport. Open the **World** menu. You can choose **Airports** and then Chicago O'Hare Intl. - Runway 27R. This brings you to the beginning of the runway (see page 214 of the *Pilot's Handbook*).

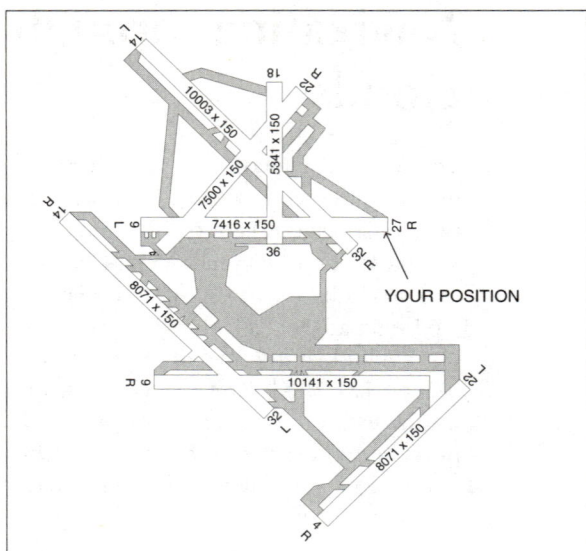

Let there be darkness

The next thing we shall do is to put the sun out. We shall fly by night. Open the **World** menu and select **Set Time and Season**.

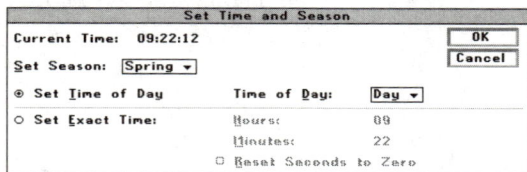

The Set Time and Season dialog box

You can now change the time of day and/or the season. The first line shows the present (simulator)

time. You can change the season on the second
line. Click on **Set Season** or press **S**. We shall select
Autumn. We shall specify the exact time by clicking
on the **Set Exact Time** button or by pressing **E**. Then
type **22** behind **Hours** and **00** behind **Minutes**.
Then click on **OK** or press **Enter**. It is now 10
o'clock in the evening sometime in autumn.

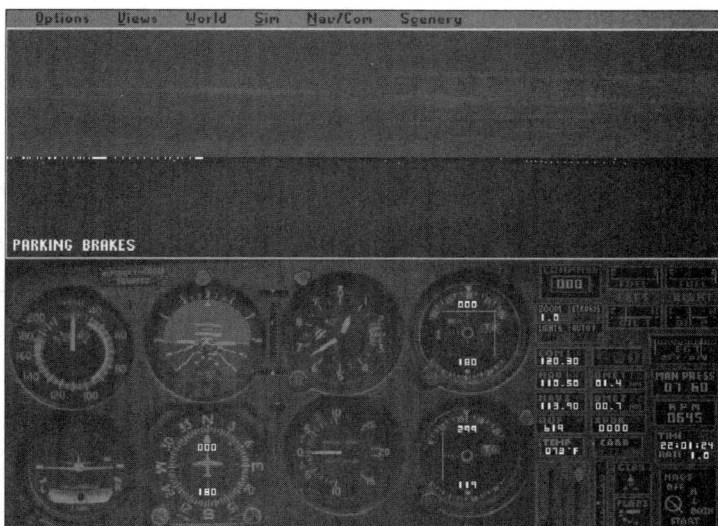

It's as dark as night

You will immediately notice that the instrument
panel is lit up in red. You can switch the lighting on
and off by pressing the **L** key. Try it. When you look
out of the window, you will see the stars and the
blue illumination of the taxiways. When we are flying in the clouds shortly, the lighting on the outside
of the aircraft may be troublesome as it is reflected
from the clouds. You can switch off the **strobe** lights
by pressing **O**.

In fact the light area in front of the aircraft should
not be there (landing light - error in the Flight
Simulator). You can see how that light shines by
looking at the aircraft from the side.

And some clouds of course

We have to make it as authentic as possible, so we
shall add some clouds. You learned how to do this
in the previous chapter. Open the **World** menu and
select **Weather**. We shall create a think cloud layer
in the **Clouds** section. Behind **Base**, type **1000** and
behind **Tops** type **10000**. Behind **Coverage** type
Overcast. Keep in mind when creating clouds, that
the specifications refer to height above **sea level**.
Thus, we have just specified that the clouds begin at
1000 feet above sea level. The airport lies at an altitude of 667 feet, so that the clouds will begin at a
little more than 300 feet above ground level.

And the wind

When you leave the Create Cloud Layer box, you
return to the **Weather** dialog box. Click on **Winds**
or press **W**. Then select **Create**. Ensure that the very
first option, **Wind Aloft**, is activated. You can now
specify the direction and force of the wind aloft.
Behind **Base**, type **0** and behind **Tops**, type **15000**.
Behind **Speed**, type **25**. The **Direction** will be **320**.
Thus, we have specified that the wind aloft will be a
northwesterly with a force of 25 knots. We now
have to specify the **Surface Wind**. Activate this
option (second line) by clicking on it or by pressing

W. Behind **Depth**, type **500**. This means that the surface wind blows up to an altitude of 500 feet above the ground. There the wind aloft settings come into force. Behind **Speed**, type **15** and type **300** behind **Direction**.

```
                    Create Wind Layer
○ Wind Aloft - MSL, True                         [  OK  ]
⦿ Surface Wind - AGL, Magnetic                   [Cancel]

Type:              Steady ▾

Depth (ft):        000499
Speed (kts):       015
Direction (Mag):   300
                       Light         Heavy
Turbulence:         1  2  3  4  5  6  7  8
                    ▲
```

The surface wind

Thus, the surface wind is also northwesterly with a force of 15 knots. You can also specify some turbulence on the bottom line if you want to make it really difficult for yourself.

Preparations in the cockpit

We have now unleashed the weather. It is now advisable to make some flight preparations so that you won't have to be so busy shortly after you are airborne. You can then pay more attention to the actual flying. One of the things we can do now is to tune the radios to the settings we shall need for navigating. To do this, you will first have to plan the flight route. On our **flight plan** (the form which we filled in to let Air Traffic Control know who we are and which route and altitude we are planning to fly), we requested a route from Chicago directly to the Roberts VOR and from there on to the Champaign VOR.

Therefore, we can tune in the first VOR to the
Chicago O'Hare VOR: 113.9 MHz and we can also
set the radial. The course from the Chicago VOR to
the Roberts VOR is 188 degrees. You can select this
for both the first and the second VOR. Specify the
frequency of the Roberts VOR for the second VOR:
116.8 MHz. Thus, for the first part of the flight, you
can use the Chicago VOR and as you approach the
Roberts VOR, you can use that one. We are now
almost ready to go. Air Traffic Control tells you that
your transponder code is 2105.

The transponder

The transponder is a transmitter in the aeroplane. Its
signals are received by the Air Traffic Control radar.
By specifying the code that Air Traffic Control gives
you, it will know exactly where you are and where
you are going. The transponder on our instrument
panel is at the right-hand side, next to the ADF
radio. It shows **XPDR**.

The transponder

Have you found it? If you have a mouse, you can
specify the code **2105** in the familiar way. You can
also press **T** to activate it and change the first number by pressing the **+** or **-** keys. The second number
can be changed by pressing **T** twice, and so on. You
can also use the **Nav/Com** menu to make these settings.

Here we go again

Get ready to go. Air Traffic Control gives you its blessing (and last sacrament).

We climb immediately into the clouds, to 4000 feet, on a course of 270 degrees. The clouds begin almost straightaway, so keep a close watch on your instruments. Hold a course of 270 degrees and climb to 4000 feet with an airspeed of 100 knots. While you are doing this, you will hear a broken acoustic signal and a white/blue light appears on the instrument panel. This is from the landing system on another runway. Pay no attention to it. You can also switch the sound off by pressing **Q**. When you reach 4000 feet, the Air Traffic Control informs you that the route you requested is too busy and they have an alternative route for you. The new route is as follows: you can fly from your present position to the Joliet VOR and then on to the Bloomington VOR and then to Champaign.

A new route

Examine your map to see if you can find the beacons. The Joliet VOR has a frequency of 112.3 MHz. You can tune your first VOR radio to this. To fly there directly, first look at which radial you are on at this moment. Therefore turn the OBS until a TO indication is displayed and the needle is in the middle of the dial. You will see that the course will be something like 202 degrees (depending on how far you have already flown) to the beacon. Therefore, change course by turning left to fly towards the beacon. The DME indicates the distance to the beacon. Air Traffic Control gives you permission to climb to 8000 feet.

You see that you have become very busy here in the clouds. Fortunately, you can press **P** to take a breather and get organised. Practising does help. You can now set the second VOR to the frequency of the next beacon. This is 108.2 MHz for the Bloomington VOR. The course from Joliet to Bloomington is exactly 200 degrees. You can select this now. You will see that, in order to follow the radial to Joliet, you will have to make corrections to the right to compensate for the wind. If there was no wind, you would have had to fly a course of 202 degrees. The wind is coming from the northwest, thus from the right, so you will have to fly a course of roughly 213 degrees to keep on the radial.

When you pass over the Joliet VOR, change course leftwards to head for the Bloomington VOR. The wind is still from the right, so you will have to correct your course a little to keep on the radial to Bloomington.

To speed things up a bit, you can check your speed in relation to the ground by pressing the **F** key and then + for the first VOR, and **F**, the **2** and the + for the second VOR.

When you get to the Bloomington VOR, use the second VOR to tune to the VOR in Champaign; we shall use the first VOR to help us in the approach to the Champaign airfield shortly. The course that you should set in your VOR to fly from Bloomington to

Champaign is 129 degrees. To find out which runway is being used, select frequency 124.85 MHz on your COM 1 radio (above NAV 1). The ATIS information is shown on the communication bar: runway 32 is in use. This runway is equipped with a so-called ILS approach system. ILS is an abbreviation of **Instrument Landing System**. This system broadcasts a radio wave along the line of the runway. This is similar to the VOR radial, but it is much more precise. In addition, there is a transmitter alongside the runway, which tells you whether or not you are at the right altitude to approach the runway - in other words, the correct **glide slope**. This information can be received using your VOR radio. You do not need to select a radial since only one wavelength is being broadcast. But it is a good help to your memory to actually select the course required to get you to the runway.

If you look at the first VOR indicator, you will see that it has not only the vertical needle which we have used up until now, it also has a horizontal needle.

The first VOR

This needle indicates whether you are under, on or above the correct glide slope. If the needle is above the middle, you are under the glide slope and you should descend less quickly. If the needle is below

the middle, you should descend more quickly to get
on to the glide slope. Since we shall use the second
VOR to fly to Champaign, we can now select the
ILS frequency on the first VOR. This frequency,
109.10 MHz, is shown on the map of Champaign
on page 213 of the *Pilot's Handbook*, in the upper
right-hand corner. The frequency is shown next to
the word LOCALIZER on the map and under ILS in
the table.

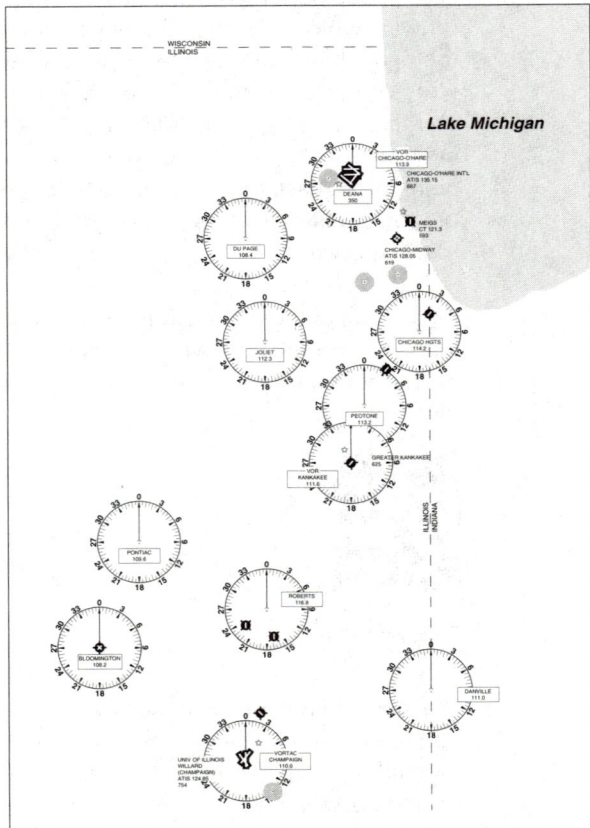

The approach procedure for Champaign

This page actually shows the entire approach procedure although you probably won't be able to grasp it because there is so much information given. A part of this resembles the exercise in blind flying which we performed in the previous chapter. The arrow on the map represents the ILS system. You will see that it is pointing to the northwest and the course is also given, 316 degrees. Therefore, this belongs to runway 32. We shall be arriving from a northwesterly direction. On the map, that means that we arrive from the upper left-hand corner, flying towards the VOR. We are thus flying in the opposite direction, on a course of 136 degrees. You will see that we pass a beacon called VEALS. Its frequency is 407, therefore it is an NDB. We have to select it shortly instead of the second VOR.

When we pass that beacon we can descend to an altitude of 2600 feet. This is shown in the upper right-hand corner of the map. After a minute, we shall fly the so-called **procedure turn**. We turn left, altering our course to 088 degrees and we follow this course for a minute. Then we turn 180 degrees to the right on to a course of 268 degrees. That is also shown on the map. Can you see it? Now pay close attention to the vertical VOR needle. It now indicates whether or not you are on the right course to the runway. It will be on the left-hand side of the dial at first because you will have to fly to the left to get on to the radial. As you come closer, it will move more to the right and you will have to switch to a course of 316 degrees. If you have to make any corrections, they should only be very small ones since the ILS is much more precise than the VOR.

Now you have to pay close attention to the horizontal needle, which indicates the required glide slope. This is displayed at the top at the moment, but will move down slowly to indicate that we are getting closer to the runway. When the needle reaches the middle, we can follow it until the runway comes in sight. It sounds quite easy but - certainly at the beginning - you will probably find it rather tricky.

That was a short explanation of the procedure we shall follow. But, in the meantime, we are still flying between the VORs of Bloomington and Champaign. When the DME instrument indicates that we are at a distance of 20 miles from Champaign, Air Traffic Control informs us that we can descend to an altitude of 3000 feet. You can begin thinking about how we are going to make the approach. Just before we reach the VOR, Air Traffic Control informs us that we may fly the ILS procedure.

Using the ADF again

We already mentioned that we would need the ADF, and this is a good moment to select it. Do you still remember how this is done? Open the **Nav/Com** menu and select **ADF**. Then select the **Activate ADF Gauge** option. This means that the second VOR will be replaced by an ADF. You can now specify 407 on the top (Frequency) line. Click on **OK** and everything should be ready.

We are now flying at a height of 3000 feet towards the VEALS beacon. When you pass the beacon you will hear the **Outer marker**. The blue light with an **O** will also light up to indicate that you are passing the marker. Now we can descend to 2600 feet. After flying this course for a minute, turn to a course of 088 degrees and keep to it for one minute. Then turn right on to a course of 268 degrees in order to fly on the Localizer, the directional part of the ILS. Lower the speed to roughly 100 knots and place the flaps in a position of 10 degrees. The speed will then fall to about 85 or 90 knots. Stay at an altitude of 2600 feet. Have a good look at the vertical needle in the ILS. When it begins to move from the left to the centre, change course to 316 degrees. Make small adjustments if necessary, a couple of degrees each time, to keep the needle in the middle. Now you have to pay attention to the horizontal needle. It will slowly move down, indicating that you are approaching the glide slope. When the needle is in the middle, press **P** to pause the simulator.

The automatic pilot

In order not to make your first time too difficult, we shall have the automatic pilot fly the last stages on the ILS. The only thing you have to do is to operate the throttle to regulate the speed. Open the **Nav/Com** menu and select **Autopilot**.

```
┌─────────────────────────────────────────────────┐
│                    Autopilot                      │
│ Autopilot Switch: │Disconnected (Off) ▾│   ┌──OK──┐│
│                   ─────────────────────   ├Cancel┤│
│ □ LVL (wing leveler)                              │
│ □ ATT (pitch and bank) Hold                       │
│ □ ALT (altitude) Hold: │009191│ ft MSL            │
│ □ GS (glide slope) Hold                           │
│ □ NAV (NAV 1 heading) Hold                        │
│ □ HDG (heading) Hold: │000.00│ Degrees            │
│ □ APR (approach) Hold                             │
│ □ BC (back course) Hold                           │
└─────────────────────────────────────────────────┘
```

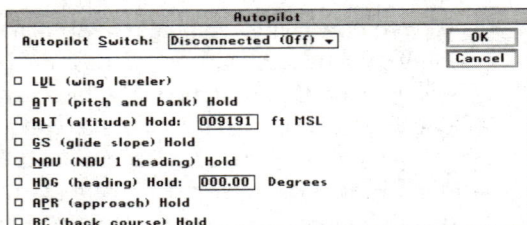

I should have known this earlier: there is an automatic pilot!

The second line from the bottom shows **APR (approach) Hold**. This enables the automatic pilot to fly the ILS. Press **P** or click on this option. Then you have to switch on the automatic pilot. This is done in the top line, **Autopilot Switch**; change it to **Connected (On)**. Then click on **OK** or press **Enter**. The automatic pilot will now fly the approach.

Before pressing the **P** key to release the pause, press **G** to lower the landing gear. As you know, you can operate the throttle by pressing F2 and F3. Try to maintain a constant speed of roughly 80 knots and keep an eye on the other instruments: you might learn something from the automatic pilot. To maintain a speed of 80 knots on the glide slope, with the flaps at 10 degrees and the undercarriage lowered, the manifold pressure should be approximately 17. When you come out of the clouds, the runway will be spread out in front of you. The approach lights should be clearly displayed.

The automatic pilot can now be fired

If you want to land the plane yourself, you should now switch off the automatic pilot. The rest should take place in the regular way which has now become familiar to you. When you have landed, take the first or second turn to the right and park the plane on the platform.

Thus, you see that it is quite straightforward to fly a small aircraft even in adverse weather conditions. You only need to think in advance about what has to be done and to keep a note of where you are. In addition, you have seen that the automatic pilot can help us in cases where we are busy with matters other than pure flying. In the following chapter, we shall deal with flying with other types of aircraft.

10 Flying the Learjet and other aircraft

Up until now we have been flying in the Cessna. It is sufficiently stable to learn how to fly and in addition it is capable of flying through bad weather, as outlined in the previous chapter. But the Flight Simulator also provides the possibility of flying other types of aircraft, as we mentioned at the beginning of this book. You can fly in a glider, in a World War 1 plane and in a modern business jet. We could write hundreds of pages about these machines, but that is not our intention here. You have already learned quite a bit, and we shall now limit ourselves to discussing aspects which deserve special attention when you climb into other cockpits.

Choosing another aircraft

Of course, the first thing you will want to know is how to get these other aircraft on to your screen. Well, that's easy enough. Open the **Options** menu and select **Aircraft**. You then can choose one of the following options: Cessna Skylane RG R182, Learjet 35A, Schweizer 2-32 Sailplane and the Sopwith Camel. We are already familiar with the first of these options, the Cessna. The second is a business jet, with two engines; the third is a glider and the last one is a biplane from the First World War. You can select one of these by moving the cursor bar to the required type and then pressing **Enter**, or by clicking on it and then on the **OK** button.

The Learjet

Let's have a look at the Learjet. Activate the second
line. A picture of the plane is shown at the bottom
of the window along with a short summary in the
Description box. If you want to know more about
the capabilities of this aircraft, activate **Performance
Specs**.

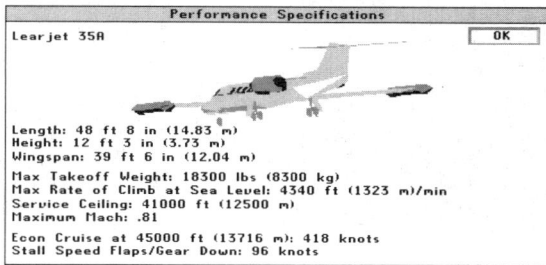

```
┌─────────────────────────────────────────────────────────────┐
│                  Performance Specifications                   │
│ Learjet 35A                                        ┌──────┐   │
│                                                    │  OK  │   │
│                                                    └──────┘   │
│                                                              │
│  Length: 48 ft 8 in (14.83 m)                               │
│  Height: 12 ft 3 in (3.73 m)                                │
│  Wingspan: 39 ft 6 in (12.04 m)                             │
│  Max Takeoff Weight: 18300 lbs (8300 kg)                    │
│  Max Rate of Climb at Sea Level: 4340 ft (1323 m)/min       │
│  Service Ceiling: 41000 ft (12500 m)                        │
│  Maximum Mach: .81                                          │
│  Econ Cruise at 45000 ft (13716 m): 418 knots              │
│  Stall Speed Flaps/Gear Down: 96 knots                      │
└─────────────────────────────────────────────────────────────┘
```

Learjet specifications

You will notice than the Learjet is quite a bit larger
than the Cessna. The plane has two engines and
can fly at high altitude, 41000 feet. You will see that
the maximum speed is shown in Mach instead of
knots. Mach 1 is the speed of sound at sea level
(1116 feet per second). Thus, in the Learjet, you can
travel at 0.81 Mach, which is 81% of the speed of
sound, meaning that you can fly at more than 600
miles per hour! Click on **OK**. This brings you back
to the Aircraft window; click on **OK** again. We are
now in the cockpit of the Learjet.

The Learjet cockpit

At first sight, this cockpit appears to be quite different to that of the Cessna. That is true to a certain extent, but if you look more closely, you will see many similarities. The familiar six flying instruments are again displayed right in front of you. The airspeed indicator is shown in the upper left-hand corner and the artificial horizon is next to it, in a larger version this time. This is a monitor screen in a real Learjet, just like the VOR and DME screen now displayed under the artificial horizon. Again you can read the ground speed, and you do not have to switch between the distance and ground speed readings. You will have recognised the altimeter and the vertical speed indicator immediately. The heading indicator is now in the spot where the Cessna turn coordinator used to be. In the real aircraft, the heading indicator is combined with the VOR in the monitor under the artificial horizon. The communication and navigation radios are again situated at the right-hand side of the instrument panel, just as in the Cessna.

To the left of the communication radio, there is a block with the following three abbreviations: **SPL, RET** and **EXT**. These are the spoiler indicators. **Spoilers** are vertical surfaces on the wing, used to disrupt the flow of air over the wing's surface. This increases the air resistance, enabling you to slow down or descend quickly when airborne, and to decrease speed when you have landed. **RET** is short for **retracted**, meaning that the spoilers are not out. **EXT** is an abbreviation of **extended**, meaning that the spoilers are out. In the Flight Simulator, the spoilers are operated by means of the / key. When taking off, make sure that the spoilers are not extended.

This time there are two throttles instead of one because there are two engines. But you operate them simultaneously (so that operation is similar to the Cessna). You can operate them separately if you wish. If you want to operate the left engine, press **E** and then **1**. For the right engine, press **E** and then **2**. There are two small red sections under the throttle handles. These represent the **reverse** section. If the throttle handles are moved into these positions, the air which comes out the back of the engines is blown forwards again, causing a braking effect. This is done by pressing **F2** when the engines are running stationary (F1).

The Learjet engine instruments

Just as with the Cessna, the engine instruments are shown on the screen by pressing the **Tab** key (does not apply to Super VGA graphic cards).

The Learjet engine instruments

The engine instruments are now displayed at the right-hand side of the screen. In the upper left-hand corner of this section, there are two instruments which indicate the revs of the left and right turbines. These figures represent the percentage of the maximum amount of revs. The temperature of the turbines is shown on the two instruments directly under these. Then, under these, the amount of revs of the so-called **fan** is shown. This refers to the blades you see when you look at the front of the engine. You could perhaps compare these to the propellers of the Cessna. These figures are also displayed next to the throttle handles if you don't have the engine instruments on screen. The dial in the upper right-hand corner shows the oil temperature, and the oil pressure is shown below this. The two instruments under these indicate the amount of fuel you are now using and the amount of fuel you still have in the tank. The 'old-fashioned' ball magnetic compass is situated in the centre post between the two cockpit windows. This post restricts your vision a little and can be turned off by opening the **Views** menu and selecting **Instrument Panel Options**.

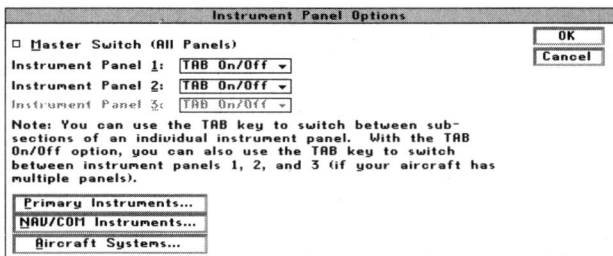

The Instrument Panel Options dialog box

The third line in this box displays the **Instrument Panel 2** option. If you change this to **Off** and click on **OK** or press **Enter**, the centre post will disappear from the screen.

What is special in the Learjet?

Which aspects require particular attention when you are flying the Learjet? The rudder is much more sensitive due to the higher speed. This means that you have to make smaller adjustments. The pure weight of the aircraft will keep you flying longer in the direction in which you are currently going. These two aspects mean that you have to think out your actions further in advance than you would do with the smaller and lighter Cessna. The two jet engines are very powerful - if you don't watch out, you will easily exceed the maximum speed. But, nevertheless, don't be afraid to give it a try. At first, everything seems to happen at an incredible speed; after a while you will get used to it and then you can have a lot of fun.

Gliding

The following aircraft you can choose is a glider, the **Schweizer 2-32**. It is a so-called two-seater, with places for two people. Open the **Options** menu and select **Aircraft**.

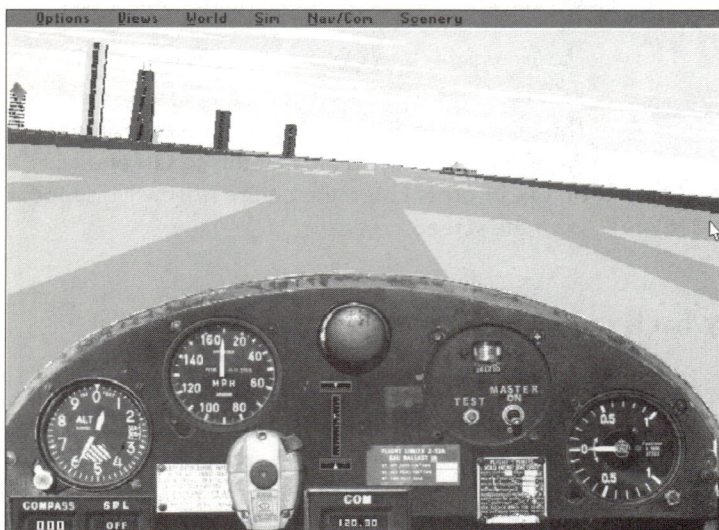

The glider dashboard

You will now see that the horizon is rather squint. This is because a glider only has one wheel, in the middle under the body or fuselage of the aircraft. The plane is therefore resting on this one wheel, and balancing further on one wing tip. You will notice immediately that the instrument panel is a good deal more simple than the panels in the other aircraft we have flown. The altimeter is displayed at the left-hand side, with the airspeed indicator next to it; this shows miles per hour instead of knots. The vertical airspeed meter is displayed at the extreme right of the instrument panel. In a glider, this is generally referred to as the **variometer**.

How do we get airborne?

In order to glide, we have to get airborne in one way or another. In real aviation, this is done by being pulled by a winch or by being drawn by another aircraft. Of course, this is not possible in the Flight Simulator, so we have to come up with another solution.

One way of doing this is to begin in the Cessna or Learjet. Once you are airborne, simply change aircraft.

Another way of doing this is to open the **World** menu and select **Set Exact Location**. You can then type the required height behind **Altitude** and you begin your flight. It is then just as if you have been pulled into the air by another plane. Let's try that.

Gliding above Germany

We shall pretend that we have been lifted into the
air above Augsburg airport in Germany. Open the
World menu and select **Set Exact Location**. Behind
North/South Lat. type **N048 26** and behind
East/West Lon. type **E010 56**. Behind **Altitude** type
5000. When you click on **OK**, you will suddenly be
5000 feet above the airfield. You will begin to fall
immediately. It will take a few seconds before you
can stabilise the aircraft. The southern part of the
airfield is specially reserved for landing gliders.
Make sure you don't stray too far from here. The
speed at which you make the least descent is
around 60 miles per hour, so try to maintain this
speed. This can only be done by changing the pitch
of the plane since you do not have an engine.
Another strange experience is that you only hear
the rushing of the wind, otherwise it is completely
silent.

Thermals

In principle, a glider will always come down.
However, if you fly through air which rises more
quickly than the glider descends, this will keep the
glider in the air for quite a while. Where is this type
of air to be found? One possibility is to fly through a
so-called **thermal**. This is air which rises due to the
fact that the sun warms up the earth's surface, but
not to the same extent at all places. Dark areas,
such as ploughed fields for example, absorb more
warmth than surrounding meadows which are lighter. This warmth is then released into the air. This air

becomes warmer than the surrounding air and rises. If you come into this rising air stream with your glider, you will also rise. Let's see if we can find one.

Open the **Options** menu and select **Situations**. A long list of options is presented. Move the cursor bar down and select **Sailplane - Thermal Soaring**.

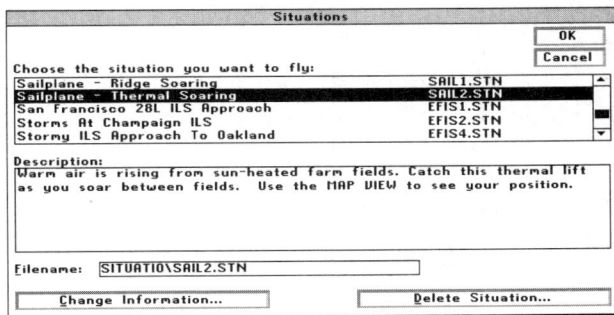

```
┌─────────────────────────────── Situations ────────────────────────────┐
│                                                          ┌─────────┐   │
│                                                          │   OK    │   │
│                                                          ├─────────┤   │
│  Choose the situation you want to fly:                   │ Cancel  │   │
│  ┌──────────────────────────────────────────────────────┴─────────┐▲│ │
│  │Sailplane - Ridge Soaring                    SAIL1.STN           │ │ │
│  │Sailplane - Thermal Soaring                  SAIL2.STN           │ │ │
│  │San Francisco 28L ILS Approach               EFIS1.STN           │█│ │
│  │Storms At Champaign ILS                      EFIS2.STN           │ │ │
│  │Stormy ILS Approach To Oakland               EFIS4.STN           │▼│ │
│  └────────────────────────────────────────────────────────────────┘   │
│  Description:                                                          │
│  ┌────────────────────────────────────────────────────────────────┐   │
│  │Warm air is rising from sun-heated farm fields. Catch this thermal lift│
│  │as you soar between fields.  Use the MAP VIEW to see your position.│   │
│  │                                                                  │   │
│  │                                                                  │   │
│  └────────────────────────────────────────────────────────────────┘   │
│  Filename:  ┌─────────────────────────────┐                          │
│            │SITUATIO\SAIL2.STN            │                          │
│            └─────────────────────────────┘                          │
│  ┌─────────────────────────┐       ┌─────────────────────────┐       │
│  │ Change Information...   │       │ Delete Situation...     │       │
│  └─────────────────────────┘       └─────────────────────────┘       │
└───────────────────────────────────────────────────────────────────────┘
```

The Situations dialog box

The darker, 'browner' fields provide the rising air-streams. Look at your variometer to find out where the strongest air currents are and make turns in that area. When you can no longer rise on that air-stream, fly to another area where you hope to find a thermal. To gain some help in this matter, you can press the **Num Lock** key to produce a map of the area on the screen.

Thermal soaring

In the meantime, don't forget to keep an eye on
your altitude and the distance to the airfield which
is on the southwest side of the hill. After all, you
want to come down safely and conveniently again.
If you land somewhere in the middle of a field, you
will have to be collected and the glider loaded onto
a trailer. There are better ways of spending a few
hours - flying for example! Are you getting the hang
of it? Gliding can be a really pleasurable sport.

The Sopwith Camel

The Sopwith Camel is an aeroplane which is very suited to playing the Simulator games. If you like, you can connect two computers to one another by means of a cable or even a modem if the distance is great, and you can go flying with a friend. Consult the Simulator manual to find out exactly how this works. Keep in mind that if you are linked via the modem, it will cost your parents a fortune if you are airborne for too long!

Flying in formation

Formation Flying is one of the interesting games you can activate. Open the **Options** menu and select **Entertainment**. Then choose **Formation Flying**. You can then select one of seven different programs. The idea of this game is to follow the plane in front of you at close distance, whilst avoiding many obstacles at the same time. When you activate this option, the Cessna is automatically selected for you, so if you want to fly the Sopwith Camel, you have to make this selection yourself.

Advanced skipping

Crop Duster

Crop Duster is another interesting piece of flying
entertainment, although it may not be very sound in
environmental terms. Crop dusting refers to spreading insecticides from a plane. You have to cover the
field as efficiently as possible. You can switch the
dusting on and off by pressing the **I**.

Who ate the crops?

When you are dusting, the quantity used is shown under the word **Smoke** in the small box at the right-hand side of the screen. You will obtain the highest score by doing it quickly and by covering the ground using as little insecticide.

That was it

As you see, the Flight Simulator has very many possibilities. The program is not only great fun, it is also educational. We have not been able to discuss all the complicated facets of the Flight Simulator, but nevertheless you have made the first steps on the way to becoming a pilot. You also know how the Flight Simulator menus work; don't be afraid to try

out all kinds of manoeuvres, nothing can go wrong.
If things do not seem to work as they should (as you
hoped), consult the manual for extra information.
Perhaps your parents or another expert will be able
to give some advice.

If the flying bug has really taken hold of you, you
can always pay a visit to the local flying (gliding)
association; maybe you can even make a real flight.
Lots of success and many happy landings!

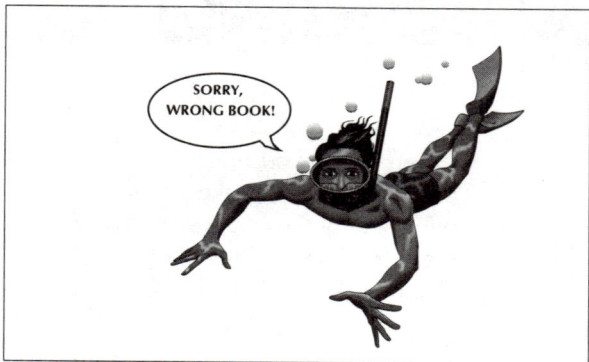

Appendix
Terminology

ADF   ADF is short for **Automatic Direction Finder**. This is a radio receiver in your cockpit which receives signals transmitted by a radio beacon on the ground, an **NDB**. An instrument needle indicates the direction of the beacon you have selected. To fly there, you have to change your course until the needle points straight forwards, towards the beacon.

AGL   AGL is short for **Above Ground Level**. If, for example, an instrument shows that you are flying 1000 AGL, this means you are flying 1000 feet above the ground.

Aileron   Ailerons are the movable parts on the back of the wings. The ailerons move in opposite directions when activated, so that the one wing produces more lift and the other less, making the plane hang squint in the air. The plane then makes a turn. When you move the joystick or control yoke to the left to make a left turn, the aileron at the left is raised and the aileron at the right is lowered. Use the ailerons in conjunction with the rudder to make a controlled, coordinated turn.

ATC   ATC is an abbreviation of **Air Traffic Control**. This keeps track of aircraft movements by means of radar, supplying information so that aircraft do not get too close to one another.

ATIS   ATIS is an abbreviation of **Automatic Terminal Information Service**. Most of the larger airports pro-

vide information about the weather conditions at
the airport and the runways being used. This information is recorded on tape which is run continuous-
ly. The pilot can receive this information by tuning
to a special frequency. The advantage of this is that
the traffic controller does not have to repeat the
same information time and again for all pilots.

Bank This means to roll in relation to the longitudinal axis
of the plane. When you make a turn, the wings
make an angle with the horizon. This angle of inclination is also referred to as the **bank angle**.

Carb Carb Heat is short for **carburetor heat**. In the carbu-
Heat retor, fuel is mixed with air to make an explosive
mixture which indeed explodes in the cylinders of
the engine, causing the propeller or blades to turn.
In flight, this mixture can become cold due to the
cooling airflow. Air almost always contains a certain
amount of water vapour. When cooled, this water
vapor can freeze, causing the carburetor to freeze
shut. Switch on the carburetor heat to prevent this.

Control This is the device which controls the elevator and
Yoke the ailerons. Turning the control yoke like a steering
wheel adjusts the ailerons, and pulling it back or
pushing it forwards adjusts the elevator. Some aircraft have a joystick instead of a control yoke.

Dead Dead reckoning is a navigation method. You keep
reckoning track of where you are by means of the course you
are on (from A to B) and the speed in relation to the
ground. You also have to take in to account the
wind at the altitude you are flying.

Drift This refers to the lateral movement of the plane caused by air currents.

Elevator The elevator is the movable part of the horizontal stabilizer at the tail of the aircraft. It is linked to the control yoke or joystick by means of rods or cables. When you pull back the control yoke, the elevator rises. This pushes the tail downwards and therefore the nose is pushed upwards. The aircraft will then climb, if you have sufficient speed.

Flaps Flaps are movable parts on the wing. They increase the lift of the aircraft and increase the air resistance so that you can fly more slowly when you want to land.

Glide Slope Glide slope refers to the information supplied by the ILS to provide vertical guidance to a plane as it prepares to land.

Ground Speed Ground speed is the speed of an aircraft relative to the ground. If a plane is flying at 120 knots true airspeed and the headwind is 15 knots, its ground speed is 105 knots.

Holding Holding is a procedure used when you have to wait in the air. Then you fly circles while waiting, for instance, for another plane to land.

ICAO alphabet In order to prevent misunderstandings, letters are not expressed as letters in aviation since some letters closely resemble others phonetically, especially over the radio. Instead, each letter has been given its own word code: A=Alpha, B=Bravo, C=Charlie, D=Delta, E=Echo, F=Foxtrot, G=Golf, H=Hotel,

I=India, J=Juliett, K=Kilo, L=Lima, M=Mike,
N=November, O=Oscar, P=Papa, Q=Quebec,
R=Romeo, S=Sierra, T=Tango, U=Uniform,
V=Victor, W=Whiskey, X=X-ray, Y=Yankee, Z=Zulu.

IFR   IFR is an abbreviation of **Instrument Flight Rules**.
                 When you are flying on an IFR flight plan, you have
                 to keep to these rules. You need this plan when you
                 are going to fly through cloud or when the visibility
                 is generally poor.

ILS   ILS is an abbreviation of **Instrument Landing
                 System**. It is an approach system which provides
                 information about the correct glide slope as well as
                 information about the course you have to fly to
                 approach the runway. You can select the appropri-
                 ate frequency on the VOR radio and the informa-
                 tion is presented on the same indicator as the VOR.

IMC   IMC is an abbreviation of **Instrument
                 Meteorological Conditions**. You fly 'in' IMC when
                 you are flying through cloud or when the visibility is
                 generally poor.

Knots   Knots are nautical miles per hour. A nautical mile is
                 defined as 1 minute of longitude at the equator.
                 This is equal to 1.15 statute miles.

Lift   In order to be able to fly, the wings have to provide
                 the necessary upwards force, referred to as 'lift'.

Localizer   The localizer is the part of the ILS which indicates
                 whether or not you are flying on the correct course
                 towards the runway.

Mach   Speed relative to the speed of sound at sea level.
              Mach 1 is equal to 1116 feet per second.

Mile   Despite increasing decimalisation, in aviation dis-
              tances are almost always given in miles. Pay atten-
              tion to whether distances are measured in **statute
              miles** or **nautical miles**. In a glider, for instance, the
              speedometer displays the speed in statute miles per
              hour. The nautical mile is used in almost all other
              cases.

MSL   MSL is an abbreviation of **Mean Sea Level**. If you
              are flying at an altitude of 1000 feet MSL, you are
              flying a thousand feet above sea level. The ground
              at that spot may be 400 feet about sea level, in
              which case you will be flying at 600 feet above
              ground level.

NDB   NDB is an abbreviation of **Non Directional Beacon**.
              This is a radio navigation beacon which you can
              receive on an ADF radio.

OBS   OBS is an abbreviation of **Omni Bearing Selector**.
              You use the OBS to select the required VOR radial.

Pilotage Pilotage is a method of navigating in which you
              determine your position by means of a map show-
              ing cities, rivers, motorways etc.

Pitch   The movement of a plane relative to the lateral axis
              (nose up or nose down).

Radial   A directional beam radiating from a VOR station,
              used to direct the aircraft towards that station.

Rudder   The rudder is the movable part of the vertical tail fin.
                  It is linked to the pedals in the cockpit. You use the
                  rudder in conjunction with the ailerons to make a
                  neat coordinated turn.

Scan   Scan is used to refer to the way of looking at the
                  instruments when flying blind, so that you can
                  obtain the relevant information at a glance.

Traffic   The **traffic pattern** is an obligatory pattern which
Pattern   has to be flown before you land. Since everyone
                  has to fly the same pattern, is is easy for everyone to
                  keep track of the other aircraft in the area. If every-
                  one were to fly around haphazardly, you would
                  have to pay attention to a much larger area to
                  ensure that you did not collide with other aircraft.

VASI   VASI is an abbreviation of **Visual Approach Slope
                  Indicator**. This refers to the lighting next to the run-
                  way which indicates whether you are on the correct
                  glide slope for landing. If you are on the right slope,
                  one light will be white and the other red. If you are
                  too high, both are white; if you are too low, both
                  are red.

VFR   VFR is an abbreviation of **Visual Flight Rules**. These
                  are the rules to which you must adhere if you are
                  not flying under IFR.

VMC   VMC is an abbreviation of **Visual Meteorological
                  Conditions**. You are flying in VMC when visibility is
                  good and you are not flying through cloud.

VOR   VOR is an abbreviation of **VHF Omnidirectional
                  Range**. This is a navigation beacon which is less sen-

sitive to disturbance than an NDB and is also more
accurate.

Index